Latin American Security Challenges

A Collaborative Inquiry from North and South

Paul D. Taylor, Editor
Senior Strategic Researcher, U.S. Naval War College

NAVAL WAR COLLEGE
Newport, Rhode Island

Naval War College

Newport, Rhode Island
Center for Naval Warfare Studies
Newport Paper Twenty-one
2004

President, Naval War College
Rear Admiral Ronald A. Route, U.S. Navy

Provost/Dean of Academics, Naval War College
Professor James F. Giblin, Jr.

Acting Dean of Naval Warfare Studies
Dr. Kenneth H. Watman

Naval War College Press

Editor: Dr. Peter Dombrowski
Managing Editor: Pelham G. Boyer

Telephone: 401.841.2236
Fax: 401.841.1071
DSN exchange: 948
E-mail: press@nwc.navy.mil
Web: www.nwc.navy.mil/press

The Newport Papers are extended research projects that the Editor, the Dean of Naval Warfare Studies, and the President of the Naval War College consider of particular interest to policy makers, scholars, and analysts.

The views expressed in the Newport Papers are those of the authors and do not necessarily reflect the opinions of the Naval War College or the Department of the Navy.

Correspondence concerning the Newport Papers may be addressed to the Editor of the Naval War College Press. To request additional copies, back copies, or subscriptions to the series, please either write the President (Code 32S), Naval War College, 686 Cushing Road, Newport, RI 02841-1207, or contact the Press staff at the telephone, fax, or e-mail addresses given.

Contents

Foreword

Sometimes lost in the deluge of attention devoted to national security challenges in the Middle East and Asia is the importance of America's own backyard, the countries and waters of Latin America and the Caribbean. Even as the United States combats terrorists and their state supporters in the greater Middle East, and even as long-range planners cast wary eyes on the growing power of China, American strategists cannot and should not neglect the threats or challenges closer to home. After all, as this volume and others point out, Latin America is a key economic partner, both a market for American products and a source of many of the goods North Americans have come to take for granted. Moreover, the distance between the two regions is not great; inevitably crises and festering problems in Latin America lead to such problems in the United States as illegal immigration. Conversely, the American struggles against al-Qaʻida and other transnational threats may bring unwanted attention to places like the tri-border region as terrorists transit or seek refuge.

Newport Paper 21, *Latin American Security Challenges: A Collaborative Inquiry from North and South,* helps reopen the door to serious analyses of the relationship between Latin American national security issues and American strategic interests. The monograph consists of an introduction and conclusion and three substantive essays analyzing specific issues facing Latin America. The first builds upon the concepts of failed states and borderless regions to suggest how criminals and perhaps terrorists can find refuge and perhaps support in localities outside the control of states. The second essay provides a solid introduction to the interconnection of economic behavior and the national security threats facing both Latin American governments and the United States. The final essay speculates on the interest of China in the region, with particular attention to the potential roles played by immigration and Chinese ownership of firms charged with operation of both access ports to the Panama Canal.

It is our hope that this work will help reinvigorate sound thinking about U.S. policies toward Latin America and encourage closer cooperation between strategists and scholars in both regions. Such cooperation would provide real benefits to the national security communities and military establishments in the United States and many critical Latin American countries.

Finally, we are especially pleased with the quality of the authors represented in *Latin American Security Challenges.* The editor, Ambassador (retired) Paul D. Taylor, is a longtime policy and diplomatic practitioner, and expert on the region, now affiliated with the Naval War College. Geoffrey Wawro and Lyle J. Goldstein are professors in the Strategic Research Department of the Naval War College, with expertise in Latin America and China, respectively. Dean Alberto R. Coll, Dean of Naval Warfare Studies, initiated this project and graciously contributed his thoughts in the introduction. Professor Wawro teamed with Julio A. Cirino and Silvana L. Elizondo of the Centro de Estudios Hemisféricos, while Professor Goldstein collaborated with Rear Admiral Guillermo R. Delamer (Argentine Navy, Ret.); Jorge Eduardo Malena of the Catholic University, Buenos Aires; and Gabriela E. Porn of the Centro de Estudios Hemisféricos on their chapter.

With good fortune and hard work on all sides, the international and interdisciplinary nature of this project may serve as a positive model for future collaborations.

PETER DOMBROWSKI
Editor, Naval War College Press
Newport, Rhode Island

Introduction

ALBERTO R. COLL

Two major trends in recent years have altered the context of discussions of security issues in the Western Hemisphere and made new assessments imperative.

The first trend is the erosion of the euphoria of the early 1990s, when the apparent success of elections in most countries of the Americas seemed to herald a new democratic era, and market-oriented economic reforms promised greater prosperity throughout the region. Regrettably, the past decade has seen a profound disillusionment, as the promises of freedom, prosperity, and greater social and economic progress have not been realized at a rate sufficient to convince citizens that their societies are on the right path. In some Latin American countries, in fact, indexes of economic and social development are stuck where they were fifteen years ago.

The other major development, brought about by the events of September 11, 2001, is an increased preoccupation on the part of the United States with terrorism as the premier security threat. While terrorism has given the Bush Administration an overarching rationale for organizing its thinking about U.S. security, the rest of the countries in the Americas do not ascribe the same priority to it, and all of them are troubled by the impression that terrorism has diverted American attention from more pressing problems in the region. These different appreciations make more important than ever collaborative efforts to assess security challenges, especially when they arise in the Western Hemisphere, close to home.

The work published in this volume represents an important effort by scholars in Argentina and the United States to share assessments of security challenges and options available to governments throughout the Americas to address them. It grew out of conversations and correspondence between Vice Admiral Carlos Luís Alfonso (Ret.), Director of the Center for Strategic Studies of the Argentine Navy, and me and furthered the collaboration over many years in which Argentine naval officers studied and served as fellows at the U.S. Naval War College. Admiral Alfonso and I agreed that a fresh look at security issues was needed in light of a radically changing environment and that, working together, Argentine and U.S. scholars could develop assessments and policy prescriptions that could be stronger than either group could produce alone. The result is a set of assessments from North and South as researchers in Argentina and the United States have grappled to reach shared judgments and policies that make sense at literally both ends of the hemisphere. As a complement to this volume being published in English by the U.S. Naval War College Press, the Center for Strategic Studies of the Argentine Navy plans to produce a version in Spanish.

The three papers featured in this volume treat different aspects of security issues in the Western Hemisphere. Their topics were determined by a process in which Argentine and U.S. researchers queried potential readers in the policy-making communities of the two countries for suggestions of pressing concerns. They then compared the lists that were developed and agreed to work on themes that were of interest to governmental consumers in both countries. While the primary audience, then, is policy makers, I believe the analyses contained herein will interest scholars and students as well.

Separate sections at the end of the volume describe the scholars who prepared the papers and the institutions that collaborated on the overall effort. The project also received invaluable support from the office of the U.S. Chief of Naval Operations.

This work comes at a time when a hemispheric appreciation has evolved that the security problem is broad and multidimensional. The Organization of American States, in the Special Conference on Security held in Mexico City in October 2003, identified a diverse set of threats, concerns, and security challenges to stability and democracy ranging from terrorism, crime and corruption; to extreme poverty, HIV/AIDS and other diseases; and to the possibility of access, possession, and use of weapons of mass destruction and their means of delivery by terrorists. The current research similarly views broadly the causes and consequences of security threats and the measures needed to address them.

Julio A. Cirino and Silvana L. Elizondo of the Centro de Estudios Hemisféricos and Geoffrey Wawro of the U.S. Naval War College start their analysis of "Latin America's Lawless Areas and Failed States" recalling that U.S. Secretary of Defense Donald Rumsfeld, at a regional security meeting in Santiago, Chile, in November 2002, expressed concern to his counterparts from other countries in the Americas about the twin problems of "ineffective sovereignty" and "ungoverned areas." Rumsfeld asserted that Latin American governments had an obligation "to exercise sovereign authority throughout their national territories" to prevent the spread of "ungoverned areas," where "narco-terrorists, hostage takers and arms smugglers" could operate with impunity and "destabilize democratic governments." The researchers examine the tri-border region of Argentina, Brazil and Paraguay, Colombia and Suriname as well as certain distressed, anarchical urban areas. They explore the notion of weak or failed states as well as "lawless areas" in which the authority of the nation state is absent and the possibility that the more states erode, the easier it will be for terrorists to root themselves in them. These situations pose considerable dangers to both Latin America and the United States.

Cirino, Elizondo, and Wawro propose from their analysis a two-track approach to hemispheric security. They argue that every effort should be made to penetrate, expose, and destroy terrorist cells. At the same time, the hunt should be accompanied by a kind of subtle nation-building, because only when governments achieve effective sovereignty over their entire territories will they be safe from exploitation by those who threaten security.

In a related paper, Paul D. Taylor of the U.S. Naval War College examines "The Security Implications of Poor Economic Performance in Latin America." Citing recent, discouraging economic results in most countries of Latin America, he explores the consequences for support for democracy, internal security, migration, and relations between Latin America and the United States. While he recognizes the negative effects on security that may flow from factors other than economic hardship, such as corruption and lack of effective political participation, he has shown that the overall consequences of poor economic performance harm security within Latin America and the ability of Latin American governments and Washington to work well together to improve security. An additional vexing problem with long-term consequences is the skewed distribution of income that afflicts most countries in the region. Taylor offers a set of recommendations that governments in Latin America and the United States simultaneously could employ to address current security, diplomatic, economic, and trade problems. While arriving at these conclusions from a direction different from Cirino, Elizondo, and Wawro, Taylor reinforces their emphasis on effective nation-building as key to improved security.

Argentine Rear Admiral Guillermo R. Delamer (Ret.); Lyle J. Goldstein of the U.S. Naval War College; Jorge Eduardo Malena of the Catholic University, Buenos Aires; and Gabriela E. Porn of the Centro de Estudios Hemisféricos assess "Chinese Interests in Latin America." They start by examining China's new and more dynamic diplomacy. They see this effort as part of a strategy aimed at developing new markets while also promoting a policy of "multipolarization." As a region geographically distant from China, Latin America had received little notice from Beijing. To the extent that China does focus on Latin America, it reflects the fact that fourteen countries in the Americas continue to grant diplomatic recognition to the Republic of China (Taiwan), and Beijing is concerned about Latin American votes in the United Nations on human rights and other issues. A major factor motivating Chinese interest is undoubtedly commercial, with exports from China to Latin America reaching almost $7 billion in 2001. The researchers identify, though, a number of reasons why further growth in commercial relations between China and Latin America may proceed slowly.

They explicitly examine several developments that have been identified as possessing potential security implications in Latin America: investments of Hutchinson Whampoa, a Hong Kong–based company, to operate both access ports to the Panama Canal; triads or transnational criminal organizations related to China; and illegal Chinese immigration and Chinese presence in the tri-border region. While recognizing a need for continuing assessment, the researchers conclude that present Chinese activities in Latin America are neither large in scale nor threatening.

Taken together, these essays represent an assessment that is more valuable than the sum of its parts. By incorporating the results of Argentine and U.S. thinking on security issues, the papers provide a series of richly multifaceted perspectives. They do not agree with one another in every respect, but the consensus they represent is the more remarkable and useful because of the diverse and independent approaches that were employed to produce them. For any policy maker or scholar interested in the Americas, I commend them enthusiastically.

A chief mission of the Naval War College since its founding in 1884 has been to promote interaction by its faculty with international military, government, and academic leaders. This enables our faculty to stay closely connected with developments in other countries, and to study those developments from an academic, analytical perspective independent of whatever policies the Administration of the moment is pursuing. One of the benefits of this strong tradition at the College, reinforced over the years by all Naval War College presidents, is obvious: a student body that is better informed and better capable of discussing complex international issues affecting U.S. strategy and policy. Throughout Latin America, Asia, Europe, and the Middle East, our faculty are hard at work trying to understand the world, and trying to explain America to the rest of the world. This collection of perceptive essays is the latest outstanding example of this fine tradition.

CHAPTER ONE

Latin America's Lawless Areas and Failed States
An Analysis of the "New Threats"
JULIO A. CIRINO, SILVANA L. ELIZONDO, GEOFFREY WAWRO

At a regional security meeting in Santiago, Chile, in November 2002, U.S. Secretary of Defense Donald Rumsfeld expressed concern to the assembled South American defense ministers about two twinned problems: ineffective sovereignty and ungoverned areas. Latin America's elected governments, Rumsfeld said, have an obligation "to exercise sovereign authority throughout their national territories" to prevent the spread of "ungoverned areas" where "narco-terrorists, hostage takers, and arms smugglers" can operate with impunity and "destabilize democratic governments." He might have added, "and arm for attacks against the United States." For much of the Bush administration's anxiety has to do with the relative facility with which Islamist terrorists, including Hezbollah, Hamas, and al-Qa'ida, can establish themselves in the big cities, provincial capitals, and ungoverned areas of South and Central America. There are six million people of Muslim descent living in Latin America; 1.5 million live in Brazil (which contains more Lebanese Arabs than Lebanon itself), and seven hundred thousand reside in Argentina. The rest of Latin America's Middle Eastern emigration is scattered, with the largest concentrations in Venezuela, Colombia, Paraguay, Chile, Peru, Honduras, and Bolivia.[1]

This joint project, involving the U.S. Naval War College's Strategic Research Department, the Argentine Navy's Center for Strategic Studies, and the Center for Hemispheric Studies Alexis de Tocqueville, recognizes the urgency and importance of these common concerns, and seeks to establish and analyze the relationships that exist among Latin America's "weak states," "failed states," and "accomplice states" and the actual conditions that give rise to what we call "lawless areas." The actual lawless areas (*areas sin ley*) that we investigate in this research reside in the Triple Frontier (*triple frontera*) of Paraguay, Brazil, and Argentina, much of Colombia and its border zones, and the small state of Suriname. There are others—in Ecuador and Peru, for example—but we address the most alarming cases, and our conclusions apply to every lawless area, a term popularized by the Center for Hemispheric Studies Alexis de Tocqueville as early as 2001.

We also investigate distressed, anarchical urban areas. The best examples of this phenomenon are, of course, the *favelas* in Rio de Janeiro and São Paolo. Less famous but no less perilous are the *villas miserias* around Buenos Aires, the *pueblos jovenes* around Lima, and every other sprawling shantytown in South-Central America that evades the control of local and national authorities, thus creating "enclaves" that, in the Brazilian case, have become "parallel states" beyond the reach or remit of the legal government.

Although objective evidence of failed or failing states is plentiful, we have, in some instances, taken the ideas of Robert Rotberg as a jumping-off point in the charting of a topic that is little discussed by analysts in our region. Almost all of the cases that Rotberg mentions refer to Africa, which has different political and cultural underpinnings than Latin America. Thus, when the time comes to explain the "roots" of the failed state in our hemisphere, the answers lean more toward corruption than problems with state creation and legitimacy, as is the case in much of Africa.

We conclude by examining the issue of whether or not to employ Latin American armed forces to control lawless areas, a delicate matter for the democracies in the region. We end by suggesting a number of strategies to cope with Latin American lawless areas.

Seeking Answers to the Terrorist Threat

The relatively new transnational terrorist threat, with its bases in obliging accomplice states, has taken much of the air out of the heady, optimistic talk of a peaceful, interdependent "global village" and deflected attention back to the old nation-state.

In Afghanistan in 2001 and afterward, the United States made clear that every nation-state is responsible for developments inside its borders, and that ineffective sovereignty and terrorist entry and activity may necessitate preemptive attacks by U.S. or coalition forces.[2] In this American interpretation, state sovereignty ceases to be an entitlement related to national self-determination and international law. Instead, state sovereignty becomes a weighty responsibility and obligation for the overall security of the international community.

In this line of thinking, two categories appear that enable us to conceptualize responses to the terrorist threat. On the one hand, we have the notion of weak or failed states—repeatedly referred to in the U.S. National Security Strategy—and on the other, areas where the nation-state is absent, areas that Secretary Rumsfeld recently deemed ungoverned zones or lawless areas.

Both concepts are closely related; they indicate a physical rooting or "territorialization" of the anti-American terrorist threat in weak, permissive states of the developing world. If, as Roger Noriega (U.S. assistant secretary of state for Western Hemisphere Affairs) said in October 2003, "strong democratic governments and prosperous societies" are the best defense against political erosion in Latin America, it stands to reason that the converse is also true. The more states erode, the easier it will be for terrorists to root themselves in them.[3]

If we review the basic literature concerning this territorialization, we can see that criminals seek to remain invisible by settling in remote areas or mingling with urban populations. Sometimes, the terrorist presence is almost virtual, and its profile is extremely low. Working as networked nodes in a global web, the eventual territorialization of these "super-empowered" terrorists presents an entirely different threat and challenge from that posed by the terrorists and "freedom fighters" of the 1970s: those operating from so-called liberated zones.

The "privatization" of global terrorists, who draw only a limited amount of support from friendly states or citizens to ensure their viability, makes it difficult to find them. Worse, their alliances with organized crime, drug smugglers, and complicit host states give them great flexibility, a regular cash flow, and actual territory where they are safe from pursuit.

The offensives against Afghanistan and Iraq—and attacks on other fronts in the "Global War against Terrorism" such as Yemen, Pakistan, and the Philippines—have pushed those fleeing terror groups to seek new sanctuaries from which to continue their fight. That is where the lawless areas come in.[4] For terrorists, there is a growing need to find spaces that offer the opportunity to "set up shop" in the Western Hemisphere, whether a lawless area or an enfeebled, relatively open nation-state.

A cursory glance reveals a number of Latin American areas that favor the territorialization of the terrorist threat. Some of them are in the Triple Frontier area of Argentina, Brazil, and Paraguay. Others lie on the borders of Argentina, Brazil, and Uruguay; the triple border area in Colombia, Peru, and Brazil; the frontier between Ecuador and Colombia; Panama's Darien peninsula; and Maicao in Colombia. We also identify Iquique in Chile, Chui in Brazil, and Colón in Panama as menacing gray areas. The mayor of Chui, Mohammed Kassem Jomaa, was linked by Uruguayan intelligence in September 2001 to al-Qa'ida, charges he denied.[5]

When the offending state actually offers the desired sanctuary, we speak of a new category: the accomplice state, among which we can include Suriname and perhaps Paraguay. These states are fully recognized by the international community. They have the capacity to both internalize and externalize their power, unlike failed states, but they are tolerant of illegal activities, having lax judicial systems and key political and military figures involved in criminal activities.

Defining Lawless Areas

We've adopted the label "lawless areas" to identify those regions not effectively controlled by the state and where rogue elements—organized crime and terrorist groups—have comfortably settled.

The sovereign power of the state is its ability to enforce the law and provide security for a country and its citizens. Thus, if the state is unable to enforce the law in portions of its territory, then we have the setting for a new lawless area and its entire array of illegal activities, which, importantly, have their own independent codes of conduct that function in place of national law.[6]

A perfect example of this situation was the notorious *despeje,* or "free zone," in Colombia—no longer in existence—where the *Fuerzas Armadas Revolucionarias de Colombia* (FARC) guerillas were permitted by Bogotá to apply their own force and laws to a region the size of Switzerland. On a smaller territorial scale, the bosses of the Brazilian *favelas* impose their edicts on thousands of people.

Three key elements facilitate the consolidation of lawless areas. The first element is simply the weakness of national and local political institutions. The weakness of the Latin American state is a critical issue for regional security. In the first place, it can be explained by two parallel processes: the *inability of the state to maintain the legitimate monopoly of force,* and the *corruption of many government officers and bureaucrats.*

Political-geographical factors are also at work. The evidence reveals that the Latin American border regions and specific geographical features generate favorable conditions for the creation of lawless areas. Socioeconomic factors play a role, too, including the spread of *free economic zones,* the existence of *ethnic minorities,* and the availability or absence of reliable *communications.*

Obviously the existence of these factors in varying strengths does not imply the automatic formation of a lawless area. Quite the contrary: it is the restless activities of criminals that drain the law and sovereignty from an area.

Lawless Areas: Triggering Agents

Two factors trigger lawless areas: politics and economics.

"Political insurgents" are the regional guerillas nowadays classified as terrorists.[7] Colombia is "Exhibit A," but Latin America is rife with other Colombia-like insurgencies. The Zapatistas in Chiapas are another example, as are certain Peruvian and Ecuadorian groups.

Interestingly, the Colombian insurgency altered its very nature once it started working with the drug-smuggling cartels, which it no longer just protects but controls and manages. In a typical year, the FARC earns more than half of its six-hundred-million-dollar revenue from the sale of cocaine and heroin. With their coca fields under relentless attack, the FARC, *Ejercito de Liberación Nacional* (ELN), and *Fuerzas de Autodefensa de Colombia* (AUC) paramilitaries have quietly become the United States' chief suppliers of heroin, furnishing 80 percent of the heroin that reaches American streets.[8] Meanwhile, they have dispersed their coca crops across smaller, concealed plantations and diverted massive cocaine (and crack) exports to Brazil and Europe. Guerillas who were once political are increasingly commercial in outlook; they are, in effect, "commercial insurgents." (See table and figure.)

"Commercial insurgencies" engage in for-profit organized crime without a predominant political agenda. The FARC, for example, has all but discarded its founding ideology of communism and Bolivarism in the all-consuming quest for money. To maximize income from illegal activities, these groups tend to interact with the public sector. At first, they corrupt select officers or bureaucrats; then they gradually undermine the entire system.

Both political and commercial insurgencies require lawless areas in which to operate. Each type of insurgency has distinguishing traits.

Political insurgents like the FARC or Shining Path, enmeshed in drug smuggling and sheltered by rough terrain, tend to carve out their own spaces. These lawless areas are barred to the state, which finds it difficult to overcome the geographical barriers and the fierce paramilitary resistance. In these cases, the lawless areas approximate the old guerilla "sanctuaries" of the 1970s.

The search for sanctuaries in neighboring countries, especially around Colombia, opens the way for a spillover or "regionalization" of local civil wars. Colombia's sprawling borderlands with Ecuador, Venezuela, Panama, Peru, and Brazil qualify, with varying degrees of intensity, for this frame of reference. "Narco-guerillas" carve out the enclaves from which terrorists and organized crime syndicates can operate as well.

In other cases, lawless areas spring from organized crime and venal officers and bureaucrats. Such spaces are buttressed by lax borders and regulatory systems, the corruption of local authorities, and satisfactory telecommunications. In marked contrast to the political insurgent, the economic insurgent does not seek to destroy the political power, but merely to bend it to his needs. Nevertheless, the corruption lever inexorably weakens and crumbles the host state from within. Witness the collapse of Fujimori's rotten regime in Peru.

TABLE 1
The Lawless Areas

AREA		TRIPLE FRONTIER	DARIEN	MAICAO
Frontier	2 countries		x	
	3 countries	x		
	No			x
Corruption	Local forces	x		x
	Accomplice state	x		
Political Insurgency	Local			x
	Neighbor		x	
	Internal			
	Eventual	x		
Commercial Insurgency	Not present	x		x
	Not registered			
Free Economic Zone	Yes	x		x
	No		x	
Geography	Jungle	x	x	x
	Other			
Active Minorities	Chinese	x		
	Muslim	x		
	Other			
	None			x
Armed Confrontations	Spread			
	Eventual		x	
	None	x		x

TABLE 1
The Lawless Areas, continued

AREA		LETICIA	LAGO AGRIO	SURINAME	COLÓN
Frontier	2 countries		x		
	3 countries	x			
	No				x
Corruption	Local forces	x	x		x
	Accomplice state			x	
Political Insurgency	Local	x	x		
	Neighbor	x	x		
	Internal				
	Eventual				
Commercial Insurgency	Not present	x		x	x
	Not registered				
Free Economic Zone	Yes				x
	No	x	x	x	
Geography	Jungle	x	x		
	Other			x	x
Active Minorities	Chinese			x	x
	Muslim	x			
	Other				
	None		x		
Armed Confrontations	Spread				
	Eventual	x	x		x
	None			x	

FIGURE 1
Dimensions of the Lawless Areas

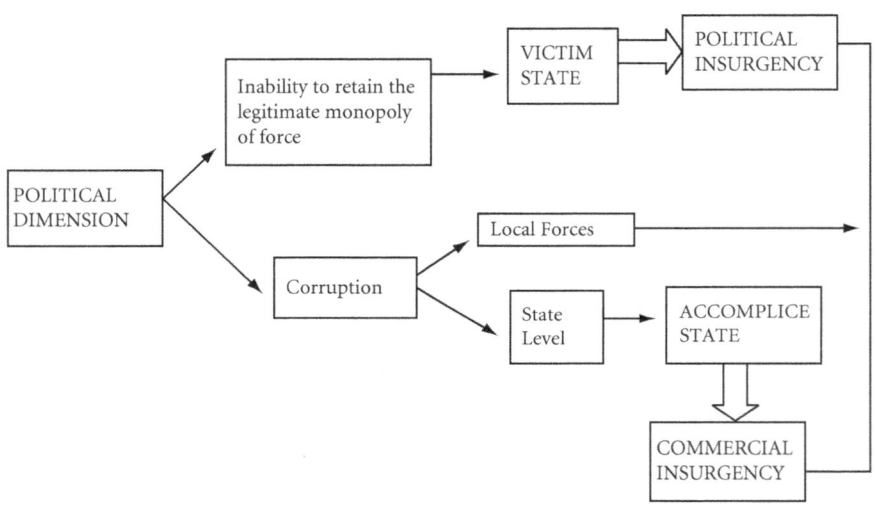

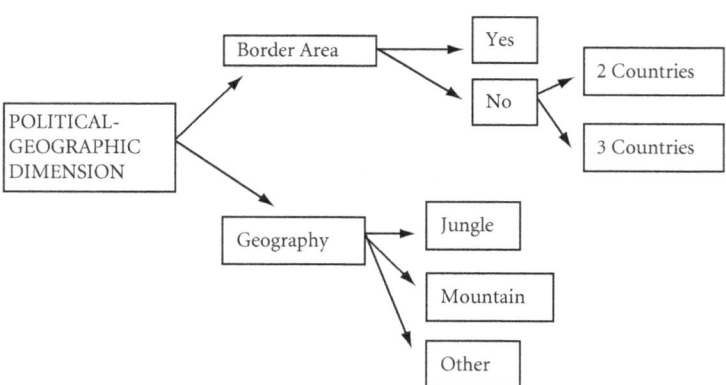

FIGURE 1
Dimensions of the Lawless Areas, continued

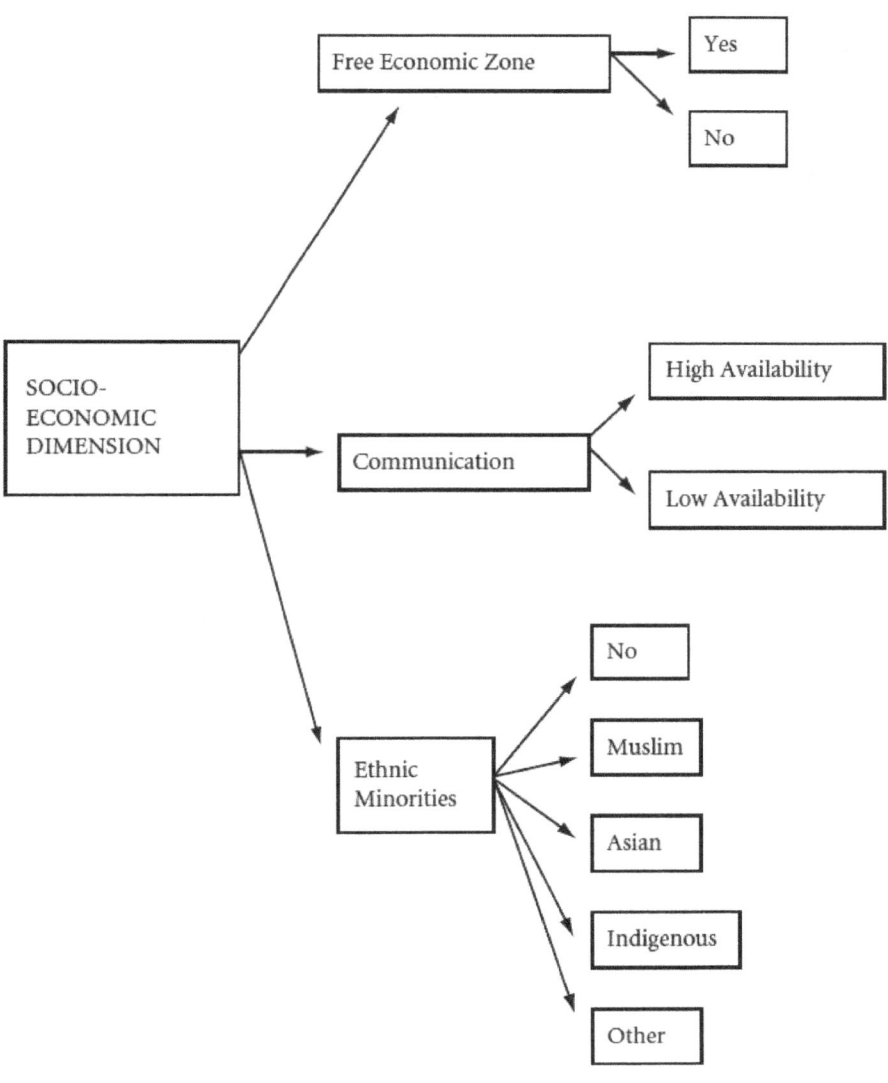

Once the lawless areas are created, whether by terrorism, corruption, or organized crime, the zones become magnets for all manner of criminals and terrorists. By and by, they become nodes in a dangerous network.

The Political Face of the Lawless Area: The Weak State

The weakness of the Latin American state stems from two factors: a global crisis of the nation-state and a regional deterioration in central state power.

On the global stage, the liberal democracies evolved since the 1970s are painfully torn by the conflicting demands of the market (lower taxes and regulation) and those of popular democracy (more social protection and services). In Latin America, the military has periodically been summoned to resolve the conflict, with mixed results. With globalization, the weakening state can be further weakened by international forces like free trade and fickle short-term investment.[9]

In the 1990s, the countries of Latin America attempted to solidify democracy and dismantle their massive welfare states. It was hoped that privatization and neoliberalism would create smaller, more dynamic enterprises. Unfortunately, neoliberalism as often as not resulted in state corruption, and a precipitous weakening of institutions and their legitimacy in the public mind. Welfare safety nets were removed, exposing millions to the shock of economic failure. The disdainful rejection of Carlos Menem by Argentine voters in May 2003 showed just how disillusioned a South American people could be with neoliberal nostrums.

On the domestic front, the continued exclusion of huge sectors of society from the production cycle generates growing demands on the state, especially in areas of security, health care, and education. Countries like Brazil, with its $350 billion foreign debt, or Argentina—bowed under $52 billion of external debt—have no cushion against these accumulating social threats. States in crisis are unable to cope with the huge demands placed on them by their needy citizens and exigent lenders. This, in turn, generates a severe governability crisis, what Favio Wanderley Reis, a Brazilian analyst, terms "Hobbesian ungovernability."[10] The phrase "refers to the deterioration of the social tissue, to the growing crime rate and urban violence, to the appearance of areas where the central state's authority has no way to assert itself, thus compromising the state's ability to provide public order and the security of its people."[11] Hobbesian ungovernability stems from two key problems that undermine the legitimacy of the state: the partial or total loss of the legal monopoly of force and systemic corruption.

Colombia is, of course, the most flagrant example of this, where the state controls only part of its territory and has surrendered control of much of the rest for four decades. Identical problems appear in Brazil, where the drug barons rule the *favelas* and administer their own judicial system. In the slums around Georgetown, Guyana, "teenage and adult civilians move about freely with AK-47 assault rifles, shotguns and handguns."[12] Similiar situations can be seen in most overcrowded Latin American cities.

Though the challenge to North, South, and Central American governments is obvious in the case of political insurgency, it is no less urgent in the face of commercial insurgencies. Think of the ease with which Rio's drug lords *(matutos)* have been able to paralyze a great city of seven million by forcibly closing schools, shops, and streets, or the way in which drug-related corruption skews the politics and public affairs of at least fifteen Brazilian states.

A second point to take into account is that challenges to the state's monopoly on armed force have been carried out vigorously, and sometimes even legitimated in the public mind. Pablo Escobar, for example, was a local hero in Colombia, where he annually donated part of his vast income to the people of Medellin. *Subcomandante* Marcos of Chiapas won wide support for his attacks against a corrupt Mexican government in the 1990s. Bolivia's Evo Morales, expelled from Congress for his vigorous opposition to the U.S.-funded counterdrug program, is today a local hero, an indigenous Robin Hood, who stands with the poor farmer (and rich *cocalero*) against U.S.-imposed eradication efforts. In 2002, Morales nearly won the presidency of Bolivia, despite massive pressure from Washington. Indeed, U.S. opposition was probably the single greatest issue in Morales's favor with Bolivian voters.[13]

Corruption shows itself everywhere in Latin America. It coats almost every level of bureaucracy, from the highest authorities, who require large sums of money to manipulate the political-administrative machine, to the small fry: customs officers, border police, and provincial and municipal officials. A searing Brazilian congressional report of 2000 identified scores of government officials involved in narcotics trafficking, including mayors, judges, police officers, two former state governors, two members of Congress, and fifteen state legislators.[14]

Although there is systemic corruption in Latin America, we are still able to distinguish between those countries where the bureaucrat allows himself or herself to be bribed to ignore certain activities (something that each of them does independently), and those where the state itself enthusiastically enters into illegal activities, using the privileges of national sovereignty and institutions to foster those activities with impunity and as much efficiency as local authorities can muster. These states, which we've denominated accomplice states, can even contrive specific laws to meet the needs of their criminal activities.

The Political-Geographical Dimension

Lawless areas are generally border zones—the greater the number of international frontiers, the better—and jungle areas difficult to access.

The border zones offer obvious advantages for political and economic insurgencies. Political insurgents prefer to set up in adjacent territories that are poorly integrated, while the commercial insurgents favor active border areas, preferring to blend in amid business and government activity and corruption. The border offers a safe place to the political insurgent and easier access to communications, weapons, provisions, transport, and banks.

For the commercial insurgency, the frontier creates a fluid, trade-friendly environment. Border controls are perfunctory in "free trade" areas, and there is a great demand for goods that are linked to smuggling, document fraud, illegal immigration, and money laundering.

For the political insurgency, terrain and topography often favor the narco-guerilla. Jungles permit him to hide massive bases and training camps, and also laboratories, plantations, and clandestine runways. The Amazon region, huge and impenetrable, is a clear example of the shelter that the jungle areas give. On all of Colombia's borders— with Panama, Ecuador, Brazil, and Venezuela—jungles cloak illegal activity, as is the case in the tri-border area. In the Triple Frontier, dozens of runways have been identified, and the Rio Parana is heavily used for illicit traffic.

The Socioeconomic Dimension

Three elements are regularly observed in the appearance of lawless areas.

First: the existence of minorities. The network of family ties that bind emigrants to their co-nationals back in the motherland is a key factor in the transnationalization of organized crime and terrorism. In the case of Latin America's Chinese minorities, their presence is notorious in the tri-border area, Colón (Panama), and Suriname. They are also active in the large Latin American cities. It is no secret that the Chinese minorities, which are particularly insular, show a close relationship with the triads for their establishment and protection.

Arab and Muslim minorities, mainly from Lebanese emigrants who fled the civil war of the 1970s, also make fertile soil for Islamist terrorism. The Lebanese communities maintain their long shopkeeping tradition, which provides convenient links for money laundering as well as the swift movement of funds to different parts of the world. There are strong Arab minorities in the Argentine-Brazilian-Paraguayan tri-border area, Maicao in Colombia, Guayaquil in Ecuador, Iquique in Chile, São Paolo in Brazil, and Chui in Uruguay.

Second: free economic areas generate a volume of business activity that encourages and hides the operations of organized crime. Several places in the hemisphere foster problems related to drug smuggling and contraband: the tri-border towns of Foz do Iguaçu and Ciudad del Este; Maicao; Colón in Panama; Iquique; and Chui, to name but six.

Third: efficient services and communications are fundamental to the economic insurgency. For this reason, most economic insurgencies gravitate toward the city. Indeed, the rural and semirural scenarios apply only in the case of drug cultivation and processing. Thereafter, real business and money laundering can only be transacted in an urban environment, where one finds banking services, telecommunications, Internet access, and a place to hide the operations. These urban settings are also needed by terrorist cells that operate in networks.

Lawless Areas and the Territorialization of Terrorism

Terrorism has traditionally been state sponsored. But since the end of the Cold War and the collapse of the Soviet Union—which had extended protection to many sponsoring regimes like Syria, Iraq, Cuba, and Libya—state sponsorship has declined in importance. Moreover, international terrorism now has independent objectives of its own and has found alternate sources of funding and logistics.

Some of these sources are provided by religious communities spread around the globe, others by alliances with organized crime, often in the lawless areas. A notorious case was the steady territorialization of al-Qaʻida in Sudan and then Afghanistan. This was particularly worrisome, for it concerned not a mere network of cells, but a network of networks. Indeed, al-Qaʻida's peculiar structure has little in common with the classical hierarchical organization of other terror groups.

The chief question, still unanswered, is why such a flexible and deadly structure as al-Qaʻida has sometimes taken a territorial form, putting many of its cells at risk "in the open." Second, after the military defeat of the Taliban regime and the flight underground of the al-Qaʻida networks, is the idea of some sort of territorialization still alive? Or have Bin Laden's network managers resolved to maintain the cells interconnected in only a *virtual* way—by using a mix of high-tech and human messengers—without trying to resettle territorially?

Even though many terrorists are anonymous and can live in the great capitals without being identified, for others the fall of Afghanistan represented immediate peril. When they had to flee, the only sanctuaries available were a handful of countries or regions: Chechnya; parts of Pakistan, Iran, and Iraq; Yemen and the Horn of Africa; certain zones in the Philippines and Indonesia; and the lawless countries and regions discussed in this article.

This issue becomes relevant for the evaluation of the future prospects of the lawless areas. If terrorists like Bin Laden choose not to territorialize their networks in the future, it is logical to wonder whether their stateless operations can maintain optimal or even good levels of efficiency. Or they can do as the FARC and the ELN have done: seize enclaves and transition from the old romantic conception of the guerilla or *jihadi* to a new, more accurate version characterized by self-financing via drug production and a cozy, mutually profitable relationship with organized crime and corrupt officialdom.

Lawless Areas and the Geography of Organized Crime

"Globalization" and "transnationalization" are words used to describe business, economic, and political trends. Increasingly, these terms also characterize crucial developments in the world of organized crime, drug trafficking, and terrorism.[15]

An example: less than ten years after the disappearance of the Medellin and Cali cartels, the Colombian government confirms the existence of over 160 networks with more than four thousand members related to forty criminal groups all over the world. A so-called Cartel of the Northern Valley *(Cartel del Valle del Norte)* is assuming a dominant role.

The cartel's expansion over the hemisphere is a reality: "Many of the Colombian groups have developed exporting routes to the south in order to reach the US or Europe from ports in Chile or Argentina. The Colombian Department of the Amazon is now the headquarters of several drug trafficking organizations, which export narcotics through Ecuador, Peru or Brazil." Brazil, of course, is a country of 175 million with a gross domestic product (GDP) of $1.3 trillion. It is the biggest and closest market for Colombian heroin and cocaine after the United States.[16]

Simultaneously, over the last decade, new criminal networks have settled in the hemisphere. The most important ones are Russian and Ukrainian syndicates that have become inside dealers in the heroin, cocaine, and weapons trade. Today they operate in agreement with Colombian, Peruvian, and Mexican drug lords, and in many cities they actually distribute drugs and arms. They have "deep pockets": in Colombia alone, drug traffickers generate an estimated two billion dollars of annual profits.[17]

The struggle against these groups is difficult, not least because the Russian and Ukrainian *narcos*—in contrast to the Mexicans and Colombians—have no preference for their own country of origin and are willing to settle anywhere. Indeed, they prefer to settle multiple cells in *dozens* of countries. Linked by computers and the Internet, with cutting-edge communication technologies and the latest encryption software, they establish diverse, secure control and communications centers.

To date, twenty-three of these centers have been detected. The key ones are in Buenos Aires, Berlin, Budapest, Geneva, London, Madrid, Miami, New York, Toronto, Warsaw, and Washington, D.C. And yet those centers are merely the tip of a deep iceberg that includes international networks such as the one existing in Peru-Ecuador, which facilitated the import of more than ten thousand automatic weapons from Lebanese merchants to the Colombian jungle.

Do such networks truly depend on the lawless areas? Not exactly: the *areas sin ley* are not indispensable. If the Latin American states were to reassert effective control over all their territory, organized crime would not disappear, but the *volume* of illegal activity would be reduced and many of the cells would be physically crushed by the reimposition of government control. Thus, organized crime groups insist on maintaining secrecy in their territorial bases, preferring always to bribe and co-opt officials rather than confront them.

Accomplice States, Victim States, and Failed States

The ineffective sovereignty exercised by a number of Latin American countries naturally exacerbates the problem of lawless areas. There is a growing recognition that weak or failed states pose considerable dangers to both Latin America and the United States. By "failed states" we—taking our cue from leading analysts like Robert H. Jackson, I. William Zartman, and Robert I. Rotberg—mean nations that cannot provide security and exercise full authority within their borders. Failed or failing states usually require outside assistance to save themselves.[18] In the latest research on the subject, most analysts agree that when the world faces a dispersed, networked, aggressive enemy, national sovereignty can cease to be an automatic entitlement and become instead an obligation to one's peers in the international community.

Most academic papers that touch on failed states assume an African milieu. But Somali, Senegalese, or Nigerian assumptions do not fit Latin America. In South and Central America, we must first grasp the concept of the weak or accomplice state, which can be applied to several regional cases. We can then consider failing states such as Colombia, and their efforts to recover. These are essentially new categories, which illustrate the peculiar realities of the Western Hemisphere.

Venezuela is perhaps the most worrisome accomplice state. President Hugo Chávez has placed his weakened regime at the service of terrorists, distributing—as reported by Linda Robinson in October 2003—"thousands of Venezuelan identity documents [*cédulas* and passports] to foreigners from Middle Eastern nations, including Syria, Pakistan, Egypt and Lebanon." Chávez employs Cuban and Libyan advisers in his security services, and provides military, logistical, and financial aid to the Colombian FARC and its kidnapping and drug-running businesses. Oddly, Chávez is buttressed by a peculiar American ambivalence. Though Washington loathes the dictator in the political sense, it sustains him economically so long as he works with U.S. oil companies.[19] With terrorists gathering on Venezuelan soil—there are radical mosques in Caracas and Hamas, and Hezbollah support cells on Margarita Island—this is dangerous hypocrisy.[20]

Other accomplice states are based on institutionalized corruption. These states are politically and economically "weak," but unlike failed states, they still exercise authority, albeit on a deliberately corrupted basis. Less ideological than Venezuela, they expend what energy they have in maintaining a modicum of public order to guard a profitable status quo, randomly colluding in illegal activities. Paraguay, Suriname, and Haiti (before the fall of Aristide) are fine examples of this. Peru descended into this category during the Fujimori-Montesinos regime, when the leaders trafficked in arms and drugs and senior generals embezzled more than thirty-four million dollars of public money during the 1990s.[21]

These accomplice states are ideal environments for organized criminals and terrorists, for they remain stable thanks to international recognition (and protection) and escape the odium and attention directed at failed states like Afghanistan or Somalia. Accorded the rights of sovereignty by the international community, they are able to keep their territory under sufficient control to ward off outside interventions. Though it is possible to characterize some parts of their territory as lawless areas where nonstate criminal or terrorist networks will settle, the states continue to function in the capitals and most of the provinces.

Faced with rampant illegal activity, authorities in the accomplice states either remain on the sidelines or actively join and promote the crime. This is generally done in one of two ways: either by passing special laws or by suborning the state's agencies, soldiers, and bureaucrats. State police or troops can be induced to remain on the sidelines by raw force: in Brazil, for example, seasoned gang members earn an average of one thousand dollars per month, compared with just four hundred dollars per month for street cops. The gangsters are better motivated and armed; they carry assault rifles, grenades, night-vision goggles, and cell phones. No wonder government police rarely venture into the *favelas;* it would be suicide to do so.[22] The chief businesses of Latin American accomplice states are weapons and human smuggling, contraband, chemical precursors, document fraud, money laundering, and drug trafficking. Among the accomplice states, we treat Suriname as a case study, while keeping under observation other cases, such as Venezuela, Paraguay, or Bolivia, where there has been a sharp deterioration in economic, social, and political stability. The unrelenting rise in corruption throughout the hemisphere increases the likelihood that victim states will evolve into accomplice states.

Victim states are those that, recognizing the problems generated by their loss of control over broad tracts of national territory, are nevertheless unable to rectify the situation. In some cases this is because they lack the military means to act decisively against a well-armed adversary. In others, it is because they cannot rein in thoroughly corrupted officers and officials. With its own armed forces deeply invested in a drug trade that supplies 20 percent of American and European demand, Haiti swings between victim and accomplice status. Jean-Bertrand Aristide's Lavalas party was sensationally corrupt and violent, as were the paramilitaries who ousted him. Whatever reformed institutions arise in post-Aristide Haiti, the disparity of wealth and resources between a "minimized state" like Haiti—where 80 percent of the population lives in extreme poverty—and the growing number of illegal transnational actors camped on Haitian soil is such that crime and corruption will likely remain the indispensable hubs of state activity.[23]

Case Studies

For closer study, we have selected three Latin American cases that we regard as exemplary and menacing. Together, these three cases—buttressed by a broader discussion of other, related cases later in the paper—give a deeper understanding of the security problems brewing in Latin America. The first case is the lawless area par excellence—the tri-border area connecting Brazil, Argentina, and Paraguay. The second case is the classic accomplice state—a sovereign state rather too easily manipulated by criminal elements—Suriname, formerly Dutch Guiana. The third case is the classic "victim state"—a country aware of its vulnerability but unable to fix it—Colombia.

Triple Frontier Area: Argentina, Brazil, and Paraguay

In the notorious Triple Frontier, we have a clear example of a lawless area initially formed by commercial insurgency that has recently begun financing terrorist cells. Though monitored by at least five different intelligence agencies—Argentine, American, Brazilian, German, and Israeli—terrorist networks have nevertheless entrenched themselves in the permissive Triple Frontier. Some activities of the tri-border Arab community have moved to Iquique in Chile, and the more notorious visitors—like Khalid Sheikh Mohammed or Osama Bin Laden—have long since abandoned the area, but the Triple Frontier remains a hive of illegal activity and a potential source of terrorist attacks. On 10 June 2004, the U.S. Treasury publicly identified a number of front companies in the tri-border area used to launder and funnel money for Hezbollah operations in Iran and Lebanon, and to extort "donations" from legitimate tri-border businesses.[24]

Politically, the tri-border area is characterized more by laxity and corruption than by overt challenges to state authority. Paraguay is the softest in this regard—indeed, so soft that it is effectively an accomplice state. The Paraguayan president and first lady have reportedly used stolen cars; Paraguay's consular agents in Miami, Panama, and Salta (Argentina) allegedly have price lists for fake visas, and Asunción's enforcement of patents and other legal controls is notoriously weak.[25] The Paraguayan government is allegedly deeply involved in smuggling activities and document fraud as well as organized crime. Weak attempts by President Nicanor Duarte to combat corruption and crime have been answered with death threats and assassination plots, most recently in January 2004.[26] The governor of the Paraguayan province surrounding Ciudad del Este is alleged to be the owner of forty clandestine airstrips used for guns, drugs, and other contraband.[27] The largest ethnic minorities in the Triple Frontier are the estimated twenty thousand Arabs and thirty thousand Chinese, two groups that make the region fallow ground for organized crime and Islamist terrorism.

In Ciudad del Este and Foz do Iguaçu, Islamists use a sophisticated network of charities and forced "donations"—20 percent of shop income—to generate cash for their organizations. Hamas and Al-Gamaat al-Islamiya are active in the Triple Frontier, and Hezbollah, whose annual operating budget is roughly one hundred million dollars, raises roughly a tenth of that in Paraguay, where there is no antiterror law to constrain donations. Al-Qaʻida has similar operations, as the post-9/11 arrest of Ali Dahroug revealed. The owner of a Ciudad del Este perfume shop, Dahroug—listed in an al-Qaʻida address book—was wiring eighty thousand dollars a month to banks in the United States, Europe, and the Middle East. Brazilian authorities estimate that six billion dollars per year is laundered in the Triple Frontier, often by inflating the cost basis of imported goods and then skimming off the surplus in foreign banks.[28] Argentine intelligence estimates that seventy million dollars of uncontrolled cross-border transactions occur every day. A senior U.S. State Department official called the region (in late 2003) "a black hole. . . .of terrorist financing."[29] U.S. Southern Command estimates that Islamist terrorist groups raise between three hundred million and five hundred million dollars per year in the Triple Frontier and the duty-free zones of Iquique, Colón, Maicao, and Margarita Island.[30] Imad Mugniyah—the alleged organizer of the 1983 Beirut embassy and Marine barrack bombings, the 1985 TWA hijacking, the Khobar Towers bombing of 1996, and the Buenos Aires bombings of 1992 and 1994—is believed to have established terrorist cells in Ciudad del Este and nearby Encarnación. His clients in the Triple Frontier may include Assad Ahmed Barakat, whose "Barakat clan" oversees much of the Hezbollah fund-raising and has wired at least fifty million dollars from Ciudad del Este to Lebanon. The Barakats, the U.S. Treasury noted in June 2004, "have used every financial crime in the book to generate funding for Hezbollah." Paraguayan police have seized correspondence between Barakat and the Lebanese Hezbollah leader Hassan Nasrallah. Nasrallah's letters thank Barakat for his support of Lebanese children orphaned by their fathers' suicide attacks.[31] In view of this suggestive material, the statement of the *Grupo 3+1* (Brazil, Argentina, Paraguay, and the United States) at the 3rd Inter-American Conference Against Terrorism that they had detected "no terrorist activity or dormant cells in the triborder area" leaves room for further detective work. (The North Americans at the El Salvador meeting did not share the sanguine view of their South American colleagues.)[32]

The outright elimination of empty spaces, lawless areas, and collapsed states would not necessarily end the terrorist and criminal threats. Almost all of the activities related to terrorism and organized crime take place, to varying degrees, in large urban centers. There is usually a well-oiled relationship between the operatives in urban centers and those settled in lawless areas, so that an active fight against criminal activities and terrorists at a specific geographical point can momentarily break the circuit but not end the problem. The solution requires complex, phased approaches that we will describe below.

Suriname's "Cocaine Highway"

Suriname stands as one of the most intriguing and challenging cases in this investigation. Information and reporting on Suriname is scarce, and the Netherlands evinces little interest in its former colony of "Dutch Guiana."

A small country of 160,000 square kilometers—the size of the state of Georgia—Suriname has a population of just 437,000, but its geographical position places it in a privileged position: facing the Caribbean as well as Europe and the United States. It borders Brazil, Guyana, and French Guiana. Because of its colonial heritage, Suriname is also linked to the former Dutch East Indies (now Indonesia), which, as we shall see below, has fostered a Surinamese al-Qa'ida link to Jemaah Islamiyah. Suriname's urban areas are concentrated in the northern part, near the coasts. To the south, where it shares a densely forested border with Brazil, towns and villages are scattered, making this zone ideal for clandestine airstrips.

Suriname received its independence from Holland in 1975. The parliamentary government installed that year was removed in 1980 by the so-called sergeants' coup. One of the sergeants would become the strongman in Suriname: Desi Bouterse. Though he has had mixed fortunes—successively challenged by insurgencies ("the Jungle Commando") and putsches ("the telephone coup")—he is now a colonel, controlling much of the cocaine traffic that flows to Europe and the United States, as well as illegal arms traffic from the Suriname armed forces to the FARC rebels in Colombia. A military faction led by Bouterse won Surinamese elections in 1996, forming a government with several ministers accused of drug and arms trafficking.

Suriname has been linked to the Colombian cartels for more than twenty years. Initial ties were forged in 1982 by Henk Herrenberg, who resurfaced in 1999 as Suriname's ambassador to the People's Republic of China (PRC), where the Suriname armed forces procure much of their weaponry. In Beijing, Herrenberg is accused of selling Surinamese passports to Chinese citizens.[33] There is probably an al-Qa'ida presence in Suriname because of the large Lebanese community. Indeed, in November 2003, the *Washington Times* reported that Latin American–based U.S. law enforcement agents had detected "a documented movement of Al-Qaeda" in an unnamed country. That country was probably Suriname, which—in the same article—the U.S. agents dubbed an "emerging terrorist threat." Thirty-five percent of Suriname's population is Muslim, they reasoned, "with a historical nexus to Indonesia, the home of Jemaah Islamiyah, which is affiliated with al-Qaeda and responsible for the [2002] Bali bombing."[34]

In 1999 a curious collapse of the currency—the Suriname guilder—occurred when a Surinamese shipment of 700 kilograms of Colombian cocaine was confiscated by the Dutch police at Schipol Airport in Amsterdam. Apparently, the Suriname government's need to cover the thirty-five-million-dollar loss wiped out the country's entire foreign exchange reserve. The embarrassing rout of the currency helped elect Ronald Venetiaan president over Bouterse's disgraced candidate in August 2000. With assistance from the Netherlands, Venetiaan has implemented a new fiscal and economic control program.

For Brazil, the persistence of Suriname's arms and drug trafficking constitutes a regional problem, for, as the U.S. State Department recently asserted in its *International Narcotics Control Strategy Report,* the Surinamese police are running a profitable arms-for-cocaine operation with the FARC and any other buyers who present themselves: one kilogram of cocaine per automatic weapon.[35] The UN's Drug Control Caribbean Coordination Mechanism has also noted "a growth in Suriname's regional role in drug trafficking." In past years, drugs had only been a local problem. Today criminal organizations from Russia, Ukraine, Turkey, Nigeria, and Colombia operate freely in the country. Desi Bouterse and his son Dino allegedly run the operations of the so-called Suri Kartel, which trades with a number of Colombian groups. Dino had previously worked in Suriname's Brazilian embassy, where he was expelled for criminal abuses of his diplomatic immunity.

In August 2002, questions were raised as to how the Suri Kartel's operations would be affected by the activation of Brazil's Amazon Region Radar Surveillance System (SIVAM), which theoretically monitors all flights traversing the Amazonian region. It is common knowledge that the cartel uses small and medium planes to fly from Suriname to Colombia and back, making two stops in the Amazon forests. Yet it remains an open question what form of interception Brazil will employ. Presidents Fernando

Henrique Cardoso and Luiz Inácio Lula da Silva have pushed for an automatic shoot-down law (and the Brazilian Congress has passed one), but Brasilia has hesitated to implement such a draconian measure because of U.S. opposition. (If Brazil does implement the law, the United States—protective of international flight conventions—will block the export of critical airspace control equipment.)[36] If ever enacted, more aggressive Brazilian countermeasures will force the drug lords to a long, complicated detour, probably over Venezuela, which will immensely complicate the logistics of their operations.[37]

Suriname's close relationship with the PRC is notable. In July 2002, a delegation of the Chinese Army High Command made a trip to Suriname to establish a jungle combat training center. If this initiative broadens, Chinese troops could be placed in Suriname and the trafficking of Chinese arms would be even more fluid than it already is.

Many of the above findings have been confirmed or enriched by court documents in the trial of Leonardo Dias Mendonça in the Brazilian state of Mato Grosso in 2002–2003. The documents, signed by Judge Antonio Veloso Pelejera, outline in detail the operations of the drug smugglers on the Colombia-Suriname-Brazil circuit.[38]

In brief, the drug-smuggling operations move between bases and runways in Colombia's Barranco Minas, Suriname, and Mato Grosso. They are key components of the FARC financing scheme—hence U.S. Attorney General John Ashcroft's repeated efforts to extradite Dias Mendonça to the United States.

The accused in the case are Leonardo "Leo" Dias Mendonça and Osmar Anastasio. Leo was the boss of the group; Osmar was one of the pilots who made regular use of the cocaine air corridor.[39] Osmar confessed that he collaborated in smuggling into Brazil 327 kilograms of cocaine, which were confiscated at the *fazenda* (ranch) "Coro Forte" in the state of Mato Grosso. The ranch is owned by Ceibal de Padua Santome, who subsequently confessed that he had supplied aviation fuel for the trip from his ranch to Colombia.[40] Osmar also described in detail the flights that transported the cocaine from Colombia to Suriname. The flights went twice a week or every other week, depending on demand. The planes were loaded with a dozen fifty-liter gas cans to extend their range. Each flight carried about 250 kilograms of cocaine, and the two pilots were paid a total of fifteen thousand dollars U.S. The plane's owner was paid thirty-five thousand dollars. The crew would leave Brazil at 1400 to reach Colombia after dark. At daybreak the next day, they would depart for Suriname.[41] With each landing in Colombia, they paid ten thousand dollars to the FARC, which operates and taxes the airfield in Barranco Minas.[42]

Usually the planes departed Brazil from São Miguel do Araguia (state of Goias); sometimes they left from clandestine airstrips in the state of Mato Grosso. Loaded with fuel for twelve hours of flight, they flew seven hours to Barranco Minas in Colombia. There they loaded cocaine and more fuel; then they flew seven hours to Suriname. Other times the planes left from Brazil to Suriname, where they loaded packs of U.S. dollars, flew on to Colombia, and returned to Suriname with a large cargo of cocaine: one-kilo bags of cocaine packed in thirty-kilo cartons, as many as the plane could carry.[43] Osmar Anastasio maintained that Leonardo Dias Mendonça was a business partner of Desi Bouterse in the cocaine-smuggling operations. Dino Bouterse was known as "the Commander." The Dutch police added that Leonardo and the Bouterses regularly traded the cocaine ($2,500 per kilo) for automatic weapons and heavy machine guns, which they then delivered to the FARC. Melvin Linscheer, chief of Suriname's intelligence, reportedly directed Leo to clandestine airstrips, including an abandoned military airfield called "Kamp 52." Another defendant testified that Etienne Bourenveen—a Suriname Ministry of Defense official—gave Leo five hundred Chinese weapons from army stockpiles, which were then delivered to the FARC.[44]

For its part, Brazil has responded to the threat with beefed-up federal police operations along its entire northern border. To their dismay, the Brazilians have discovered even tiny Amazon villages overrun and used by the FARC or other drug traffickers. The frontiers with Venezuela, Suriname, and Colombia are regarded as wide open, as is almost inevitable given the vast spaces. Brazil's border with Colombia alone runs 1,645 kilometers, and the FARC has planted coca and poppy plantations all along it. "We are increasing the control and repression efforts to our maximum capacity to prevent Brazil from becoming a transit country for so many types of drugs," a senior Brazilian police official told O Estado de São Paolo in April 2003. It is probably too little, too late; the federal police, like so many organs of the Brazilian state, are suffering through a financial crisis and, by their own admission, cannot keep pace with the traffickers.[45]

Overall, Suriname represents a specific kind of Latin American threat: the accomplice state infiltrated by "official criminals" eager to place their powers and immunities at the disposal of mafias, traffickers, and terrorists.

Colombia: Perennial Victim State

Colombia, of course, is the "market maker" for Surinamese crime, and the troubles in Colombia constitute the most glaring threat to hemispheric security. The conflict has thus far defied geographical containment, spilling beyond Colombia's borders into Darien (Panama), Lago Agrio (Ecuador), Peru, and the region bordering Venezuela. Brazil, deeply worried by the crisis, has thus far proven helpless to prevent "spillover" into the Amazonian region. Forty percent of Colombia's national territory—including cities and rural areas—is controlled not by the government, but by the guerillas or paramilitaries, a lack of control exacerbated by the softness and permeability of the five border areas. Although Colombian president Alvaro Uribe Velez is struggling to reverse the trend, the recent record of Colombia has been that of a nearly failed state without control over large parts of its territory.

There are, of course, historical and military reasons for this. Since the 1970s, the left-wing guerillas of the FARC and the ELN and the right-wing paramilitaries of the AUC have aimed to conquer and consolidate territorial enclaves. Today there are roughly eighteen thousand FARC guerillas, five thousand ELN paramilitaries, and twelve thousand AUC paramilitaries in action. All of the militias have gradually subordinated their political programs—communist revolution on the left, defense of the elitist status quo on the right—to an economic program of cocaine and heroin production, supplemented, in the case of the paramilitaries, by generous contributions from cattle ranchers. In this way they are scarcely distinguishable from the approximately 162 foreign and domestic drug cartels based in Colombia.[46] Colombia produces 580 tons of cocaine a year; rebels like the FARC live not from popular support, but from an estimated eight hundred million dollars in annual drug revenues. The right-wing AUC gleans at least 70 percent of its funding from cocaine and heroin.[47] To bolster these revenues, the guerillas, paramilitaries, and cartels have physically chipped away at the Colombian state to make room for coca and poppy plantations, which have increased from thirteen thousand hectares in 1983 to two hundred thousand today. Murders and kidnappings to dissuade the reimposition of state control have risen proportionately: thirty-four thousand homicides and three thousand kidnappings last year, and 1.5 million terrified refugees driven from their villages and towns to city slums by the narcos. No less than 60 percent of the world's kidnappings occur in Colombia, and the refugee influx has an evil byproduct: it facilitates FARC efforts to "urbanize" the civil war, by infiltrating guerillas into the *villas*.[48] The kidnappings exert obvious pressure on the victims, but also on families and friends, enabling the kidnapper to coerce an entire village, clan, or region.

Unable to enforce the law or even preserve the lives of its citizens, Colombia is marked by these high levels of violence and a culture in which powerful organized crime elements converge with insurgent movements. At the same time, the justice system disappears under the rule of *plata o plomo,* "money or lead." The entire economic infrastructure of the country is under near-permanent attack: roads, airports, oil pipelines, and electricity grids. FARC and ELN attacks on oil facilities are part of a broader strategy to bankrupt Bogotá (which must repeatedly rebuild the damaged assets) and eventually annex oil- and coffee-producing regions. The guerillas have wrought an ecological holocaust over the years, cutting 2.4 million hectares of tropical rain forest, spilling 2.2 billion barrels of oil into Colombia's rivers, and dumping an estimated six hundred million liters of pesticides and chemical precursors into Colombia's soil and water every year. On top of extensive spraying in the U.S.-supported Plan Colombia, the damage is devastating.

The guerillas flagrantly misuse Colombia's 9,200 kilometers of international borders, using the frontiers with Ecuador, Peru, Brazil, Venezuela, and Panama for rear-area logistical support and so-called mobility corridors beyond the reach of the Colombian military. Foreign firms—especially Americans—have been targeted as collaborators. Last year, poor Colombia shed 8 percent of its GDP this way, at a time when every *centavo* is needed to develop the country.[49]

Though operating separately, the two left-wing armies—FARC and ELN—and the right-wing AUC share a basic strategy: by terrorism, illegal financing, diplomatic overtures to sympathetic foreign governments and NGOs, and attacks on the Colombian armed forces, they seek to create a failed state that would leave them free to pursue their illegal activities. With the Colombian state and military in tatters, the legal economy paralyzed, and the populace cowed and terrified, the guerillas would be free to consolidate their territory and expand their business and power. For the FARC, all of this is accomplished under the guise of "popular sovereignty" in so-called freedom areas. Mayors, judges, and governors are slaughtered to undermine the state and give the guerillas a veneer of political ideology: they are selflessly returning power to the people, constructing a "New Colombia" from virtuous "Bolivarian circles."[50] The paramilitaries have been no less ruthless in the opposite direction: they slaughter hundreds of peasants every year, seeking to tear the FARC and ELN up by their roots. Until now, the guerillas have had a relatively easy time of it. All of them established their bases in the wild, thinly populated Colombian southeast, where labs, trails, camps, and river transport have been easily concealed beneath 135,000 square miles of tropical forest that are impervious to satellites or infrared sensors. The guerillas had little to fear from the pre–Plan Colombia Colombian military, which lacked the sensors, helicopters, and aircraft needed for the mobile-strike operations now under way. The FARC also benefited from overt Venezuelan support. With several bases on the Venezuelan side of the 1,400-mile border, the FARC has more than just a safe haven for operations in Colombia. According to the *New York Times,* it sometimes receives close air support from the Venezuelan air force in battles with the AUC paramilitaries. Using cocaine and drug money, the FARC regularly purchases guns and ammunition from Venezuelan officers.[51]

Carlos Castaño's AUC is more complex. Sensing Uribe's resolve, Castaño tried to "come in from the cold," proclaiming a cease-fire (vis-à-vis the government) in December 2002 and urging the AUC's regional armies or "blocks" to cease their drug operations and revert to their original mission of holding the line against FARC revolution.[52] Castaño, who vanished under mysterious circumstances in May 2004, was reacting to the "9/11 effect": ever since the attacks of 11 September 2001, guerillas and para-militaries alike have been shunned as terrorists. The FARC and the ELN have been denied visas by a previously supportive European Union, and Washington has blacklisted doz-ens of paramilitaries previously viewed as allies in the struggle against the FARC.[53] Still, AUC grandees like Castaño and Salvatore Mancuso, who have obvious political ambi-tions in a revived and pacified Colombia, can probably not disarm and neutralize local paramilitary commanders eager to cash in before order is restored. Castaño is believed to have been kidnapped and murdered by his own militias, who feared that he would reveal AUC drug operations to the Americans.[54] Moreover, many doubt Castaño's sincerity. Many of his paramilitaries work *with* the FARC to grow and traffic drugs. As the dissi-dent paramilitary commander "Rodrigo 00" declared in July 2003, "The AUC [con-tinue to] talk like narcos, live like narcos and act like narcos."[55] Also, though several thousand paramilitaries demobilized in late 2003, it was discovered that their numbers concealed a significant number of FARC kingpins, who purchased "AUC franchises," took amnesty as ex-paramilitaries, and thereby won legal immunity to launder drug money and take title to land used for drug cultivation.[56]

Against these mounting threats, Colombia under Uribe fights for its soul. It has not de-generated to the level of a failed state in the sense of classic models such as Somalia, Af-ghanistan, and Sierra Leone.[57] Rather, the Colombian state, still threatened by the corrosive power of corruption, is struggling to recover its balance, especially in the fight against the guerillas. Among the mass of voters, the idea of a Colombian nation still persists, and the continuity of a strictly civilian governing elite ensures a degree of stability. Furthermore, Uribe has refreshingly "formalized the idea that the fight is waged by *fighting*, not by talking" and has forced the Colombian military to take back previously written-off regions, like the Colombian-Peruvian Amazon.[58]

President Uribe is winning the guerilla war with an apparently effective two-track strategy: increased military pressure twinned with psychological/humanitarian opera-tions to provoke guerilla desertions and reintegrate the resultant deserters into civil so-ciety. On the military track, operations have intensified thanks to U.S. assistance. In the first five months of 2003 alone, the Colombian armed forces killed or captured 1,416 guerillas, a historically high rate of attrition. A U.S.-assisted "decapitation strategy" re-sulted in the death or capture of at least six senior guerilla leaders in 2003. In June, Uribe swore in ten thousand "peasant militiamen" to guard the villages, and aerial fu-migation has cut Colombia's coca production for the first time in ten years. (Figures on poppy production are less clear.)[59] American officials estimate that by 2005 the spray program will reduce Colombia's coca harvest to less than one-fourth the acreage planted in 2000. The Colombian vice president told the U.S. Senate in June that all ille-gal drug crops would be eradicated by 2006.[60] This is probably overly optimistic. In fact,

Colombia's drug producers have proven resilient. The *narcos* have transitioned from vast plantations targeted for spraying to smaller, isolated farms planted with more potent strains of coca that yield more cocaine from fewer plants. They have created new markets in Brazil and Europe, which now consume as much crack and cocaine as the United States, further spurring the illicit demand that eats away at the Colombian state.[61]

On the humanitarian track, Bogotá's reinsertion program—begun by Pastrana in 1998, but quadrupled by Uribe—had fomented 720 FARC desertions by June 2003. With a "reinsertion" budget of $14 million, Uribe aims for no less than six thousand desertions this year: one-fifth of the guerillas' total strength. Though he is far from his target, he has provoked more desertions in the past nine months from the FARC, the ELN, and the AUC than in the previous three *years* combined. There are military and philosophical reasons for this: communist ideologues resent the hypocrisy of the FARC struggle, which is now focused on drugs. Carlos Plotter, a FARC officer who turned himself in under Uribe's program, declared in June 2004 that "the humanism that attracted me to the FARC [in the early 1990s] is gone. Nothing is worse than a guerrilla with money."[62] Yet most FARC deserters are simply teenagers who have known only the relative peace of the years before Uribe and are unprepared for the efficiency of the army's attacks or the ferocity of the AUC's mopping-up operations.[63]

Still, the Colombian military continues to reorganize. Uribe has promised to insert the Colombian military into all of the nation's 1,098 municipalities, cease all cooperation with the right-wing AUC, and increase the army from sixty thousand to one hundred thousand troops by taxing the wealthy, conscripting high school graduates (previously exempt), and conscribing peasant militias. Predictably, the FARC has turned its attacks on the new militias to demoralize them. There are other hurdles to cross: the straitened nation is spending just 1.9 percent of GDP on defense, and assigning just 54 percent of its military personnel to the guerilla war, just 6 percent to border patrol. Whereas countries like El Salvador, Pakistan, and Syria have one troop per square kilometer, the ratio in Colombia is one-to-eight, which tends to relax pressure on the narco-guerillas.[64]

We would most accurately classify Colombia as a victim state, with only some of the characteristics of a failed state. Energetic U.S. intervention, which comes in the form of military and economic aid, has staved off the worst effects of drug smugglers, terrorists, and occasional Venezuelan support for the FARC. Authors that specialize in the subject of failed states—Hellman and Rattner, Rotberg, and Woodward—have found that such outside intervention is the quickest way to prevent collapse. As Rotberg puts it, "Strengthening weak states against failure is far easier than reviving them after they have definitively failed or collapsed."[65] Since the start of Plan Colombia in 1999, Bogotá has become the third-largest recipient of U.S. military aid, after Israel and Egypt:

$3.2 billion to date.[66] Although it is impossible to say what would have ensued without Plan Colombia, American aid has clearly helped turn the tide. Still, Colombia needs far more than just military aid to recover from a civil war begun more than fifty years ago, in 1948.[67]

Colombia is a democracy under siege from guerilla groups that terrorize the civil population, subvert institutions, and ignore the constitution. Provinces like oil-rich Arauca in the northeast have become virtual free-fire zones, with a murder rate of 160 killings per one hundred thousand citizens—double that of the 1990s, and thirty times the U.S. rate. The popularity of the guerillas has plunged from a steady 80 percent in the 1980s to barely 2 percent today.[68] Massacres are depressingly routine in some provinces, where the FARC and paramilitaries wipe out each other's peasant growers.[69] The entire economy has been ruined by war, with twenty-eight million Colombians—60 percent of the population—living in extreme poverty. In 2003, the FARC, ELN, and right-wing paramilitaries abruptly pushed the war into indigenous areas (25 percent of Colombian territory), killing dozens of indigenous and black leaders to gain control of their land.[70] They have pushed the war into and across all of the nation's international frontiers. There are rebel camps in Panama, Ecuador, and Venezuela, and fund-raising networks in Brazil that traffic in arms, drugs, and gold.[71] In late 2003, FARC agents attempted to purchase Nicaragua's entire arsenal of SAM-7, SAM-8, and SAM-9 shoulder-fired missiles, 2,116 missiles in all.[72] This might be, as *Jane's Terrorism and Security Monitor* conjectured a month before the alleged purchase attempt, an example of "Western intelligence's worst nightmare…that Islamic militants will make common cause with indigenous revolutionary movements and narcotics-traffickers [like the FARC] to pool resources."[73]

All of this adds up to a severe military and terrorist threat. However, nonmilitary strands must also be woven into the threat analysis. Bogotá's political and bureaucratic machinery—some of which lends credibility to FARC demands for a "New Colombia"—must be reconstituted on a cleaner, more efficient basis. One reason given for Colombian defense minister Marta Lucia Ramirez's abrupt resignation in November 2003 was her inability to account for three tons of cocaine taken from police storage. (Though personally innocent, the minister had never been informed of the scandal.)[74] Colombia's budget must be restrained and labor, pension, and banking laws reformed. The fight against corruption must be waged mercilessly to return credibility to the state. The military has been involved in many scandals (like that of early 2003, when Colombian army officers were tried for diverting 7,640 Bulgarian AK-47s to the AUC paramilitaries), and dozens of Colombian senators and deputies owe their seats to drug money.[75] Sanity must be restored to basic administration. The Colombian guerillas and paramilitaries receive *millions* of dollars a year in Colombian oil revenue from the

National Royalties Commission. The reason: frightened or corrupt commissioners, contractors, and local politicians channel the money to local guerillas rather than local schools and other social programs.[76]

Uribe, recognizing that judicial efficiency and official probity are necessary preconditions to any Colombian renaissance, seems to be working hard at efficiency and accountability. He has pledged 113 trillion pesos over the next four years for regional development and the creation of what his planners call a "community state," one less riven by wealth and class.[77] His handling of the Colombian army's botched hostage rescue operation in May 2003 was emblematic of the new accountability. Rather than sweep the failure under the carpet, Uribe, pledged to "openness and transparency," forced the army chief and another senior general to go on national television to explain the debacle. Similarly, when two of Colombia's elite counternarcotic companies stole an estimated $14 million in captured FARC funds in May, Uribe deliberately broadcast the scandal, to show Colombians his determination to enforce honesty in the Colombian military, police, and civil administration. Uribe is the first Colombian president to hold the army's feet to the fire: though the army had captured or killed few FARC commanders in forty years of civil war, they got five in the fall of 2003 alone, a surge attributable to the president's personal attention.[78]

Meanwhile, money must be poured into the educational system, to forge real "citizens." As Alejandro Santos Rubino—editor-in-chief of Colombia's most influential newsmagazine—put it at a Social Forum meeting in Bogotá in 2002, "Is a country in which 60 percent of the people live below the poverty line a viable country? Twenty-eight million Colombians do not know a thing about ideology, visas, economic deficits or even human dignity."[79] Uribe, new on the scene when Rubino spoke those words, recognizes the danger of this; indeed, his vaunted reinsertion program is founded on an appreciation of education and civil responsibility. Guerilla deserters are pardoned, taught to read and write, provided vocational training, and then released into society with a stipend of two thousand dollars. A nation-state is, in effect, reinventing itself.

Armed Forces and the Lawless Areas

The fight against terrorist and organized crime networks will demand technical and intelligence capabilities more than raw force. It will also require a sophisticated level of cooperation among Latin American ministries, militaries, and security services. Improved systems of regional cooperation will also aid in the fight against terror cells and criminal organizations.

Improved systems and methods cost money. Latin American defense ministers have rather too optimistically judged their region a "haven of peace" and are spending little on defense.[80] This creates opportunities for terrorists and traffickers, who have little to fear from the region's obsolete militaries. (In real dollars, the region's four major powers have reduced their arms purchases 40 percent over the past decade.)[81] It is facile to argue that Latin America's problems are not military. They are, of course, economic, social, and political, but military weakness opens the door to transnational intruders. Brazil is a good example of this. After subtracting salaries and pensions from Brazil's already-tiny twenty-nine billion *real* defense budget, the nation is left in 2003 with just five billion *reals* (US$1.7 billion) for operations and procurement. Only ten thousand of the army's one hundred thousand troops are deployed in the Amazon region, and the rest of the force is constitutionally forbidden to operate against the gangs in the *favelas* or any other internal enemies. Asked in January 2003 whether it was not time for Brazil to reform its unskilled conscript army into a smaller professional force able to cope with the new threats, defense minister José Viegas Filho replied, "No." The army, he said, must continue to function as a school of the nation, integrating "whites, blacks, mulattos and Indians."[82] Such words are probably balm to the spirits of terrorists and traffickers, who can make the most of Brazil's weakness in the Amazon—the big cities and the border areas. Against an army pledged not to operate internally and a federal police force of just seven thousand men (two thousand of whom sit in offices), criminals have room for maneuver and growth in Brazil.[83]

North and South: Different Perceptions and Priorities

Latin America remains a relatively low priority issue in Washington, whose chief hemispheric security concerns are Venezuelan oil and narco-terrorism in Colombia. Unfortunately, most other countries in the region resent these narrow, self-interested priorities. Compared with the advances in economic and trade integration, defense and security are areas in which nationalist tendencies take longer to change and where effective consensus is harder to build.

For Americans, September 11 created a turning point of sorts. With al-Qa'ida spanning sixty countries, Washington began to look more closely at endangered or embattled victim and accomplice states in the hemisphere. Facing the difficulties of engaging an organization with the characteristics of al-Qa'ida, a network of networks that snakes through several dozen countries, the United States has decided that each nation-state must take responsibility for what happens inside its borders. As British prime minister Tony Blair put it in July 2003, "The right to sovereignty brings associated responsibilities to protect citizens."[84]

In select cases—chiefly Colombia—Washington is paying more attention to Latin America. Latin America, however, deplores *this* kind of attention, for the region has quite different concerns. Brazil worries that Colombia's civil war is but a pretext for the

United States to push its military power into the Amazon and the Andean ridge. Yet Brazil has its own lawless border area with Colombia, one that threatens to spread deep into the heart of Brazil. Like the tri-border area, Tabatinga/Leticia, at the southern end of the 1,600-kilometer Brazil-Colombia border, has been a lawless area and haven for organized criminals for ten years, a market for drugs and weapons and a favorite route—along the Amazon—for the shipment of the chemical precursors needed for cocaine and heroin production in Colombian laboratories.[85] Aside from four army outposts around Manaus, the Brazilians have done little to contain the infection. With a strict policy of "nonintervention" in Colombian affairs, Brazilian outposts—isolated and poorly linked—can do nothing anyway. Though Brazil is adding thirteen jungle bases and increasing its troop strength in the Amazon region to 26,000, such a force scarcely registers in a sprawling jungle of 2.12 million square miles.[86]

In Foz do Iguaçu, Tabatinga, and elsewhere, national and regional security will be a sensitive matter for Brazil, and cooperation with the United States is neither natural nor assured. President Lula da Silva must first focus on social and economic problems. One-third of Brazil's 175 million citizens live on less than one dollar a day, and one-fifth of the population is illiterate. Da Silva's "war on hunger" will precede a war on anything else, including terrorists. His June 2003 proposal to tax international arms sales and third-world debt repayments to remove the "structural causes of world hunger" gives a glimpse of his methods and priorities.[87] Brazil also fears unchecked American "hyperpower," which might one day impinge on Brazilian interests or—in the case of Foz do Iguaçu or the Amazon—even Brazilian territory.[88] A leading Brazilian congressman has called it "a tragedy to have U.S. soldiers in South America," and Brazil's overt support for Hugo Chávez in Venezuela's December 2002 crisis was a clear signal that da Silva may view Chávez as a potential geopolitical makeweight against American encroachments in Colombia, Ecuador, Peru, Bolivia, and Chile. Similarly, Brazil's recent call for "total defense integration" with Argentina is likely to be warmly received by President Nestor Kirchner, who has publicly decried the Argentine-American "carnal relations" of the Carlos Menem years.[89]

Mexico abandoned the Cold War–era Rio Treaty in 2002, on the grounds that the chief threats to the region are not military, but social and economic. Mexico resents Washington's focus on drugs and terrorism, and its refusal to conclude a new, post–September 11 immigration agreement, relax import restrictions on agricultural products, or legalize the status of the estimated three million undocumented Mexican workers in the United States. President Vicente Fox, who began his presidency in 2000 vowing to work in tandem with President Bush, has tacked away since the Iraq War. Fox, the former Coca-Cola executive, spurned Washington's efforts to get an additional UN resolution to authorize the use of force against Saddam Hussein and looks increasingly to

Brazil and the EU, seeking membership in the G8, a permanent seat on the UN Security Council, and some "diversification" of Mexican exports, 90 percent of which go to the United States.[90] Mexico does not view terrorist cells as an urgent threat. Indeed, in October 2003, Mexico's foreign secretary publicly accused the United States—at an Organization of American States (OAS) security conference—of "seeking to militarize the OAS."[91]

In Venezuela, the ongoing struggle between President Hugo Chávez and his fractured opposition leaves Caracas incapable of defending (or unwilling to defend) its 2,219-kilometer FARC-ridden border with Colombia, or of implementing effective countermeasures against organized crime and terrorism in its own territory.[92] If Chávez—president until at least 2006—continues to stoke the civil war in Colombia, he may find himself in conflict with the United States. He tolerates fifteen FARC camps and four of the ELN, a permanent presence of up to two thousand men, and scores of kidnap victims inside Venezuela.[93] Chávez makes no secret of his support for the FARC against Colombia's "rancid oligarchs" and has even supported a FARC-modeled kidnap and extortion force called the *Fuerzas Bolivarianas de Liberacion* (FBL). There are an estimated three hundred FBL guerillas; they prey on wealthy Venezuelan ranchers and may be the core of a future Chávez resistance, should he be driven from power.[94] Chávez also exists in a curious symbiosis with Fidel Castro's Cuba. In return for fifty-three thousand barrels of Venezuelan oil per month, Castro staffs Venezuela's intelligence and paramilitary arms with thousands of operatives and advisers.[95]

In Ecuador, where another populist regime was inaugurated in January 2003, social tensions are worsening in the midst of a serious economic meltdown, occasioned in part by Ecuador's adoption of the dollar in 1999. As neighbors devalue their national currencies, dollarized Ecuador loses jobs and competitiveness. In the 2002 presidential elections, Ecuadorians faced a stark and rather unappealing choice, between a left-wing populist (a former army colonel who had led a coup against democratically elected president Jamil Mahuad in January 2002) and a right-wing populist (a banana baron accused of enslaving children on his plantations). The retired colonel, Lucio Gutiérrez, won in a ballot that *The Economist* dryly called "a choice between Hugo Chávez and Silvio Berlusconi."[96]

Gutiérrez has since embarked on a struggle against what he calls Ecuador's "corrupt oligarchy." In fact, he is just the latest example of what the University of Lima's Enrique Ghersi calls the "modern caudillos," men like Hugo Chávez, Efrain Rios-Montt, and Evo Morales, "who lead what they know will be failed revolutions in order to become democratic candidates against the system."[97] Gutiérrez is hard-pressed politically, and his armed and security forces are stretched to the limit, between the reappearance of *Sendero Luminoso* on Ecuador's Peruvian border and the FARC's presence on the

Colombian frontier, where a scant 1,600 Ecuadorian troops patrol the 400-mile border. There the FARC and Ecuadorian criminals have created another lawless area, Lago Agrio, where the FARC shelters from Colombian army offensives and barters drugs for weapons and bomb-making materials with impunity. Like other lawless areas, Lago Agrio is inhabited by criminals and *traficantes* who are better armed and motivated than the police, gendarmes, and military who oppose them.[98] Anyway, with core political support from Ecuadorian communists, radical indigenous groups, and the Maoist Democratic Popular Movement, Gutiérrez has little room for maneuver against revolutionaries of any stripe. Indeed, a FARC deserter in May 2003 told his Colombian captors that Gutiérrez has "tacitly" concluded a nonaggression pact with the FARC, permitting it bases and freedom of movement inside Ecuador in return for a pledge not to attack Ecuadorians (and perhaps a cut of the FARC's drug exports).[99] In November 2003, Colombia's president accused "rogue Ecuadorian military officers" of selling FARC rebels a rocket launcher used in a failed assassination attempt on the head of the Colombian cattlemen's association.[100] Rated Latin America's second most corrupt country in 2002 (better only than Paraguay, slightly worse than Bolivia and Argentina), Ecuador will struggle to confront its monstrous challenges in the years ahead.[101]

The Rio Group Summit of nineteen Latin American heads of state, convened in Cuzco in May 2003, summarized the troubles confronting Latin American governments. As luminaries like Chávez, da Silva, Fox, and Uribe met to discuss the problems of the region, they were drowned out by tumultuous crowds of protesters, chiefly striking teachers and bus drivers, who pushed up to the very doors of the summit, hurling abuse at Peruvian president Alejandro Toledo for his neglect of wages and living standards. Though Peru actually did well in 2003—4 percent growth and modest 1.5 percent inflation—populists argue that the benefits accrue only to the rich, a common complaint on the subcontinent.[102] Indeed Toledo's embattled government—his approval rating is down to 10 percent—is just the latest victim of a Latin American trend. Fantastic as it may seem, Alan Garcia, who oversaw Peru's wretched collapse in the 1980s, is poised for a populist comeback.

In their different ways, Peru's Garcia, Venezuela's Chávez, Brazil's da Silva, Ecuador's Gutiérrez, Argentina's Kirchner, and Bolivia's Morales all represent a rejection of the so-called Washington Consensus: free markets, deregulation, privatization, and American-backed fiscal policies. Bolivia's change of heart is perhaps the most alarming. Though Bolivia nearly eradicated coca between 1997 and 2002, its acreage has bounced back to fifteen thousand and is growing. Morales, who heads a party called "Movement Toward Socialism," describes himself as a man in "sharp conflict with globalization and capitalism," which are, in his view, "the worst enemies of mankind." These are seductive prescriptions in a country where more than 60 percent of the population lives in grinding poverty.[103] Spurred by Morales, violent street demonstrations across Bolivia in October 2003 ended with the removal of the democratically elected president, Gonzalo Sanchez de Lozada. The new president, Carlos Mesa, hesitates to act against Morales, the coca growers, and their allied, Colombian-modeled terrorist army, the *Ejercito de Liberación Nacional—Bolivia* (ELN-B). Indeed Mesa has already bowed to hard pressure from Morales, releasing a number of ELN-B terrorist suspects from jail in December 2003. This development, coupled with the surge in Bolivian cocaine production and trafficking, leaves some American officials worried that the entire nation of Bolivia is slipping toward ungoverned area status.[104]

With political instability, economic crisis, and swelling social pressure threatening democracy itself, Latin American governments are faced with a delicate dilemma. Although their security and governance problems go far beyond the question of lawless areas and the terrorist menace, these threats will assuredly expand as transnational actors linked to organized crime and terrorism and empowered by state complicity and corruption extend their activities. As state power weakens and income gaps and social exclusion widen, it is logical that drug and other crime cartels and terror networks will increase their power and capabilities. To counter such threats, Latin American nations need wide, deep reforms. Improvements in intelligence and police work, for example, are all too often undone by decrepit judicial systems that prove too corrupt to implement the work of their security agencies.[105] As often as not, the police themselves are riddled with corruption. "We have two problems," Brazilian federal police chief Paulo Lacerda frankly admitted in February 2003. "Police corruption and illegal arms traffic. The criminal is strong and powerful because he has guns to confront the police. And a police weakened by corruption becomes an easy target."[106] Where there is a determined effort to tighten up the police and check terrorism, liberal critics emerge to evoke memories of the "dirty wars" of the 1970s and 1980s. "What about the 'collateral damage' of the war on terrorism," Argentina's *Pagina 12* asked in January 2003. "Damage to the presumption of innocence, to precious human rights, to the rule of law....We may end up corroding the democratic vessel from within."[107] Nor do most Latin American militaries want to be involved in domestic policing, which distracts them from other external missions and carries high political risks.[108]

Conclusion

In the first days of his administration, President George W. Bush vowed to inaugurate a new "Century of the Americas." That ideal, talked about in his first foreign trip (to Mexico), was dashed by the attacks of 11 September, which refocused American attention on the Middle East. Unfortunately, the terrorist menace is not confined to the Middle East and Central Asia; it breeds in the slums and ungoverned areas of Latin

America. It is inseparable from many of the economic, social, and political problems of the region. There is potential for terrorist basing in all of the victim and accomplice states and lawless areas described in this chapter, as well as in others that can be hewn out of previously stable areas on short notice.

This joint paper has argued the need for a two-tracked approach to U.S.–Latin American security. Every effort must be made to penetrate, expose, and destroy terrorist cells, as well as their links to drug production and sales. But the hunt must be accompanied by a kind of subtle nation-building. At the OAS meeting in June 2003, one South American official voiced his exasperation with U.S. methods. Latin America, he complained, "has fallen off the map" for Washington, *except in connection with the war on terrorism.*[109] Latin Americans would like to see the United States relax trade restrictions and invest in its neighbors to eliminate the conditions that support terrorists and *narcos,* as well as the fervently anti-American "populist movements." These last are social and political groupings that join human rights and environmental activists, indigenous communities, a humiliated middle class, farmers thwarted by American tariffs (or cheap imports), and workers impoverished by privatization, downsizing, and deregulation. "The strategy to apprehend *Mono Jojoy* [FARC leader Jorge Suarez Briceno] is far more exciting and newsworthy than an increase in the number of classrooms," an influential Colombian wrote last year, but "the dilemma today is how to break the vicious circle between war and poverty. Should we give priority to security in order to reactivate the economy as a way to help stamp out poverty? Or should we prioritize social investments to resolve the 'objective causes' of violence and in this manner reactivate the economy?" With American backing, Uribe has plumped for the former course. Regarding the latter course, Americans are leery of investing in Latin America at a time when Latin Americans themselves refuse to invest there. It was estimated in 2003 that Latin Americans had stashed up to seven hundred billion dollars of personal savings in U.S. and European banks to preserve them from Argentine-style *corralitos* (prohibitions on personal savings withdrawals), taxes, or expropriations.[110] Needless to say, the struggle will be as long, tiresome, and thankless as similar projects in Iraq or Afghanistan. Just to raise Colombia's poorest eleven million up to the poverty line will cost an estimated 2.3 percent of GDP.[111] Such work and expenditure will be the essential underpinning for real security, let alone a "Century of the Americas."

Overall, Islamist terrorism is a minor concern for the region. That fact was driven home at the above-mentioned Rio Group meeting in Cuzco, Peru, in May 2003. There, nineteen heads of government issued a "Cuzco Consensus" that differed diametrically from Washington's. Terrorism, fiscal austerity, and drug eradication did not even make the list. Instead, priorities were reducing poverty and hunger, bolstering civil society, empowering women, promoting development, deepening democracy, freeing trade in agriculture, and strengthening ties to the European Union.[112] Conferring with foreign ministers from Latin America and the Caribbean at the OAS annual assembly in Santiago, Chile, a month later, U.S. Secretary of State Colin Powell found himself quite alone in emphasizing the "triple scourge" of "tyrants, traffickers and terrorists." His colleagues preferred to focus on a different scourge: worsening economies.[113] No wonder: Latin American unemployment and poverty are at twenty-year highs and living standards are plummeting, taking whole bands of the middle class with them.[114] Washington must consider, among its security concerns, the fact that anti-American discourse is strengthening in the hemisphere, and is indeed the glue holding together a number of strident populist movements.

To be sure, uncertainty will be the rule for the coming years in Latin America, but persistent weakness, inefficiency, and corruption—if unchecked—threaten far worse than mere "uncertainty." Indeed, we might see an avalanche of failed or failing states along the lines of Colombia. Having studied the self-financing, drug-peddling methods of the FARC, Peru's nearly extinct Shining Path is making a comeback in the jungle-clad mountains of the Apurimac River Valley and the Rio Ene region, about three hundred miles southeast of Lima. This "neo-Shining Path"—characterized by Alan Garcia in July 2003 as "the most serious threat to [Peruvian] democracy"—has already established commercial contacts with the FARC and Mexican cartels, and has adopted the FARC financing method of abduction for ransom, kidnapping sixty gas-pipeline workers in June 2003. The FARC is cooperating with Shining Path, to offset its territorial losses in Colombia with Peruvian enclaves and drug trafficking routes.[115] In Brazil's cities, FARC instructors are reportedly trading their expertise in guerilla tactics, bomb making, and mass prison escapes for shipments of automatic weapons and munitions.[116] Chile, in no danger of failing, has nevertheless become the quickest growing hub for global drug transshipments and money laundering, after Brazil. With its relatively sophisticated economy and flood of exports (30 percent of GDP), Chile provides cover and facilities for drug traffickers in neighboring Bolivia and Peru.[117] Given al-Qa'ida's recent shift to drug trafficking as a principal means of fund-raising—and its close study of FARC operations—these Latin American developments are troubling.[118]

With its growing antiglobalization, antieradication movement, Bolivia is bending under tremendous pressure as FARC and Peruvian agents already on Bolivian soil deepen their ties to international traffickers and move determinedly to create a failed state that, like pre-Uribe Colombia, would be more hospitable to drug production and terrorists.[119] Guatemala—with the biggest population and economy in Central America—has fallen into what even the normally chary UN calls "lawlessness." Nicaragua, accused of selling arms to the Colombian guerillas in January 2003, replied that it was "the victim of an organized crime operation" that somehow infiltrated army arsenals. (Perhaps for this reason, U.S. Secretary of State Colin Powell took the highly unusual step in November 2003 of requesting that Nicaragua voluntarily destroy its roughly two thousand Soviet-supplied SAM-7 shoulder-fired antiaircraft missiles lest they fall into the hands of terrorists.)[120] Simply recasting the "war on drugs" as a "war on terrorism" in no way changes the fundamentals of any such struggle, which Powell recognized when he enjoined his Central American colleagues (in Honduras and Nicaragua) to fight "corruption and mismanagement."[121] Two hundred and fourteen million Latin Americans live in extreme poverty today. Looking at the region's wretched economic growth over the past twenty years—barely 7 percent per capita—many blame the United States and the IMF, and meet America's emphasis on terrorism with indifference, or sarcasm, as in the title of Ariel Dorfman's *Chile: The* Other *September 11th,* an account of the Pinochet coup of September 11, 1973, and the subsequent repression.

Maybe it is time for Washington to implement new, deeper, sustained relations with the hemisphere. Brute force and exhortations are not working; that much is clear from Zogby and Latinobarómetro polls released in November 2003. Both indicated a doubling of Latin Americans with a negative image of the United States. In key countries, percentages of citizens with a negative view of the United States are rising: 58 percent in Mexico, 62 percent in Argentina, 42 percent in Brazil, and 37 percent in Chile.[122] Far more than rhetoric or police work, economic recovery, clean government, and an educated civil society remain the foundation stones for any final assault on terrorists and drug traffickers. The American role must be steady but discreet, to allay Latin fears of *gringo* overreach. As a Brazilian report concluded in January 2003, armed repression of terrorism is only palliative. "Correcting the distortions that currently prevail on the international scene and supporting democratic values and respect for human rights will have the most effective impact on the fight against terrorism." On the Latin American side, real dedication to regional security—in every dimension—is no less important. "If we do not have a collective and regional security policy," Brazilian academic Alfredo Valladao wrote in February 2004, "we will merely continue as the dogs barking on the side of the road, while the caravan passes."[123]

Notes

1. Martin Edwin Andersen, "Al-Qaeda across the Americas," *Insight,* 26 November 2001, pp. 20–21; "Brazil faces Tricky 'War on Terror,'" *latinnews.com,* 26 June 2003.

2. Elected governments have the responsibility to exercise sovereign authority, conferred at the ballot box, throughout their national territory. Defense Ministerial of the Americas; statement by Secretary of Defense Donald H. Rumsfeld, Santiago, Chile, 19 November 2002.

3. Roger F. Noriega, remarks at the Inter-American Defense College, 22 October 2003.

4. There are records of the settlement of al-Qa'ida cells in failed or accomplice African states, such as Sierra Leone, Burkina Faso, and Liberia. Using those bases, the terrorists started a new model for funding their activities: "conflict diamond" smuggling, with the complicity of local authorities, the support of local businessmen from Lebanon, and the involvement of the Russian mafia. Doblas Farah, "Report Says Africans Harbored Al Qaeda Terror Assets Hidden in Gem Buying Spree," *Washington Post,* 29 December 2002.

5. "Search Extends to Latin America," Stratfor.com, 19 September 2001.

6. Norberto Bobbio, *Estado, gobierno y sociedad* (Buenos Aires: FCE, 2001).

7. Steven Metz, *The Future of Insurgency* (Carlisle, Penna.: SSI, 1993): "Two forms of insurgency are likely to dominate the post–cold war world. Spiritual insurgency is the descendant of the cold war–era revolutionary insurgency. It will be driven by the problems of modernization, the search for meaning, and the pursuit of justice. The other form will be commercial insurgency. This will be driven less by the desire for justice than wealth. Its psychological foundation is a warped translation of Western popular culture which equates wealth, personal meaning, and power."

8. Juan Forero, "Hide and Seek among the Coca Leaves," *New York Times,* June 9, 2004; Juan Forero, "Latin American Poppy Fields Undermine US Drug Battle," *New York Times,* 8 June 2003; Also: a talk by Linda Robinson, *US News & World Report* Latin American bureau chief, at the Pell Center in Newport, R.I., on 1 December 2000.

9. Hans-Joachim Spanger, *The Ambiguous Lessons of State Failure,* Failed States Conference, Florence, Italy, 10–14 April 2001.

10. We understand "governability" to be the government's capacity to legitimate its decisions on the basis of an efficient undertaking of its functions. It is relevant to point to the same relationship among governability, legitimacy, and efficiency. Adrián Acosta Silva, *Gobernabilidad y Democracia—Perspectivas del Debate a Veinte Años del Reporte a la Comisión Trilateral,* available at http://www.uacj.mx/Publicaciones/noesis/adrian.htm.

11. Fábio Wanderley Reis, "Atualidade mundial e desafios brasileiros," *Estudos Avançados* 14, no. 39 (May/August 2000), pp. 14–20.

12. Foreign Broadcast Information Service [hereafter FBIS], "Guyana Probes Romanian-made Weapons Origin," ACANEFE (Panama), 25 April 2003.

13. Robert D. Novak, "Cultivating Ferment in Bolivia," *Washington Post,* 5 January 2004; Erin Ralston, "Evo Morales and Opposition to the US in Bolivia," 14 July 2002, www.zmag.org.

14. "Brazil: Control by Criminal Gangs Leading to Parallel State," Stratfor.com, 20 September 2002; Matt Moffett, "Local Battle: One Tough Mayor Shows Argentina How to Clean House," *Wall Street Journal,* 1 July 2003.

15. Matthew Brzezinski, "Re-engineering the Drug Business," *New York Times Magazine,* 23 June 2002.

16. "New Colombian Cartel," Stratfor.com, 30 April 2002.

17. Capt. Juan A. Rairan, Colombian Navy, "Colombian Narcoterrorism's Strategic Implications" (unpublished paper, U.S. Naval War College, May 2003).

18. Robert I. Rotberg, ed., *When States Fail* (Princeton: Princeton Univ. Press, 2004); Robert H. Jackson, *Quasi States* (Cambridge: CUP, 1990); I. William Zartman, ed., *Collapsed States* (Boulder, Colo.: Lynn Rienner, 1995); Jeffrey Herbst, "Responding to State Failure in Africa," *International Security* 21, no. 3 (Winter 1996–97); Gerald B. Helman and Steven R. Ratner, "Saving Failed States," *Foreign Policy* 89 (Winter 1993), pp. 3–21; Robert Rotberg, "Failed States in a World of Terror," *Foreign Affairs* (July/Aug 2002), p. 127; Robert Rotberg, "The New Nature of Nation-State Failure," *Washington Quarterly* (Summer 2002), pp. 85–96; Susan Woodward, "Failed States: Warlordism and 'Tribal'

Warfare," *Naval War College Review* 52, no. 2 (Spring 1999), p. 55.

19. Christopher Whalen, "Who Is Protecting Hugo Chávez?" *Insight,* 25 November 2003.

20. Linda Robinson, "Terror Close to Home," *US News & World Report,* 6 October 2003.

21. Lucien Chauvin, "Peruvian Army Paying a Price for Recent Role-boost by Toledo," *Miami Herald,* 1 July 2003.

22. "Crime and Politics in Brazil," Stratfor.com, 24 June 2003.

23. Scott Wilson, "Armed Attacks Increase Pressure on Haitian Leader," *Washington Post,* 18 November 2003.

24. U.S. Department of Treasury press release, 10 June 2004, "Treasury Designates Islamic Extremist, Two Companies Supporting Hizballah in Tri-Border Area"; William W. Mendel, "Paraguay's Ciudad del Este and the New Centers of Gravity," *Military Review* 82, no. 2 (March–April 2002); and Mariano Cesar Bartolome, "La Triple Frontera: Principal Foco de Inseguridad en el Cono Sur Americano," *Military Review* 82, no. 4 (July–August 2002).

25. Mendel, "Paraguay's Ciudad del Este."

26. Kevin G. Hall, "Duarte Returns Home Amid Reports of a Plot," *Miami Herald,* 27 January 2004.

27. Peter Hudson, "There Are No Terrorists Here," *World Affairs* 164, no. 2 (19 November 2001).

28. Larry Rohter, "South America Region under Watch for Signs of Terrorists," *New York Times,* 15 December 2002.

29. Philip Sherwell, "Revealed: The South American Connection," *London Sunday Telegraph,* 9 November 2003; "Islamist Terrorism in Latin America," *Jane's Terrorism and Security Monitor,* 1 October 2003.

30. "Latin America: A Safe Haven for Al Qaeda?" Stratfor.com, 4 September 2003.

31. U.S. Department of Treasury, "Treasury Designates Islamic Extremist, Two Companies Supporting Hizballah in Tri-Border Area"; Marcus Stern, "Terrorism Takes Root in Jungle of South America: Region Linked to Funds for Hezbollah, Hamas," *San Diego Union-Tribune,* 15 June 2003; Jeffrey Goldberg, "In the Party of God: Hezbollah Sets Up Operations in South America and the US," *New Yorker,* 28 October 2002.

32. FBIS, "Brazilian Police Arrest Lebanese Citizen," *ABC Color* (Asuncion), 30 January 2003; FBIS, Horacio Verbitsky, "Argentine Bill to Fight Terrorism," *Pagina 12,* 26 January 2003.

33. Brana Shute, "Narco Criminality in the Caribbean" (Georgetown University talk, Washington, D.C., 2000).

34. Nicholas Kralev, "OAS Balks at Defense Treaty," *Washington Times,* 1 November 2003.

35. FBIS, "Brazil: Defense Minister Viegas Discusses Shoot-down Law, FARC Activities," *Brasilia Air Force Command,* 20 May 2003.

36. FBIS, Marcia Brandao and Carla Benevides, "US Retaliation Jeopardizes Amazon Surveillance," *Brazilian Camara dos Deputados,* 30 April 2003.

37. FBIS, "Brazil: Defense Minister Viegas discusses shoot-down law, FARC activities."

38. Kevin G. Hall, "Brazilian Drug Lord Sentenced to 23 Years for Cocaine Trafficking," *Knight Ridder Newspapers,* 22 January 2003.

39. "Sentencia Juez Antonio Veloso Pelejero." Poder Judicial, Estado de Mato Grosso, Proceso 1015/2000, 13 January 2003, p. 1.

40. Ibid., p. 2.

41. Ibid., p. 12.

42. Ibid., p. 16.

43. Ibid., p. 18, 23.

44. Ibid., p. 46.

45. FBIS, Edson Luiz, "Brazil Steps Up Security to Fight Organized Crime on Border," *O Estado de São Paolo,* 28 April 2003; "Despite Brazil's Efforts, Colombian War Likely to Seep Across the Border," Stratfor.com, 5 March 2003.

46. Marcella, *The US and Colombia: The Journey from Ambiguity to Strategic Clarity,* pp. 8–9, 21.

47. "New Drug Gangs Spreading in Colombia," Stratfor.com, 3 April 2002.

48. "Helping Colombia," *International Herald Tribune,* 12 May 2003; Rairan, "Colombian Narcoterrorism's Strategic Implications."

49. Rairan, "Colombian Narcoterrorism's Strategic Implications."

50. See www.movimientobolivariano.org.

51. Linda Robinson, "Terror Close to Home," *US News & World Report,* 6 October 2003; Juan Forero, "Colombia's Long Civil War

Spreads Turmoil to Venezuela," *New York Times,* 1 June 2003.

52. Alma Guillermoprieto, "Letter from Colombia: Waiting for War," *New Yorker,* 13 May 2002.

53. "Guerrillas—or Terrorists?" *The Economist,* 8 December 2001; JoAnn Kawell, "Terror's Latin American Profile," *NACLA Report on the Americas* 35, no. 3 (November/December 2001), pp. 52–53.

54. Margarita Martinez, "Officials: No Proof Carlos Castaño Slain," Stratfor.com, 30 April 2004; Ruth Morris, "Colombian Paramilitary Leaders Announce Peace Talks," *Los Angeles Times,* 16 July 2003; "Colombian Appeals for Peace," *Washington Times,* 23 July 2003.

55. Scott Wilson, "Commander of Lost Causes," *Washington Post,* 6 July 2003; "Colombia: Paramilitary Rifts to Lead to Violence?" Stratfor.com, 27 May 2003.

56. Andy Webb-Vidal, "Departure of Paramilitaries Could Put the Lights Out," *Financial Times,* 15 November 2003.

57. Marcella, *The US and Colombia: The Journey from Ambiguity to Strategic Clarity,* pp. 9–10.

58. "World in Brief," *Washington Post,* 14 November 2003; Hernando Gomez Buendia, "Security: Will We See Results?" *Semana,* 13–19 January 2003.

59. "Colombia Enlists Peasant Soldiers," *Washington Post,* 17 June 2003; T. Christian Miller, "Major Cocaine Source Wanes," *Los Angeles Times,* 8 June 2003; Rachel Van Dongen, "The Right Man," *New Republic,* 16 June 2003.

60. Bryan Bender, "Visible Cracks: Narco-Terrorism in Colombia," *Jane's Defence Weekly* 40, no. 3 (9 July 2003); Guy Dinmore, "Colombia Plans to Eradicate Drug Crop in Three Years," *Financial Times,* 4 June 2003.

61. Forero, "Hide and Seek among the Coca Leaves."

62. Frank Davies, "Rebel Says He Defected over Drug Ties," *Miami Herald,* 17 June 2004.

63. FBIS, Jorge Lesmes, "Colombian Military Leaders Proclaim Guerrillas' Defeat," *El Espectador* (Bogotá), 4 May 2003; Frances Robles, "Colombian Civil War Weapon: Coaxing Guerrillas to Desert," *Miami Herald,* 16 June 2003; Rachel Van Dongen, "Colombian Rebels Abandon Arms," *Christian Science Monitor,* 28 May 2003.

64. T. Christian Miller, "Major Cocaine Source Wanes," *Los Angeles Times,* 8 June 2003; Rachel Van Dongen, "The Right Man," *New Republic,* 16 June 2003; Rairan, "Colombian Narcoterrorism's Strategic Implications."

65. Rotberg, "The New Nature," p. 94.

66. Forero, "Hide and Seek among the Coca Leaves"; Jason Hagen, "The Colombian Quagmire," *Baltimore Sun,* 8 June 2003.

67. Marcella, *The US and Colombia: The Journey from Ambiguity to Strategic Clarity,* p. 7.

68. Rairan, "Colombian Narcoterrorism's Strategic Implications."

69. Juan Forero, "Attack by Colombia Rebels Threaten Fragile Talks," *New York Times,* 17 June 2004.

70. Rachel Van Dongen, "Colombian Tribes Caught in the Middle," *Los Angeles Times,* 24 May 2003.

71. Juan Forero, "Colombia's Long Civil War Spreads Turmoil to Venezuela," *New York Times,* 1 June 2003.

72. "FARC Offer to Buy Missiles Reported," *Miami Herald,* 9 November 2003; "Nicaraguan Missile Danger," *Los Angeles Times,* 8 November 2003.

73. "Islamist Terrorism in Latin America," *Jane's Terrorism and Security Monitor,* 1 October 2003.

74. Juan Forero, "Pressure Cited as Colombian Resigns Post," *New York Times,* 11 November 2003.

75. "Colombian Officers Go on Trial on Charges of Trafficking in Bulgarian Weapons," *Semana,* 23 January 2003; "New Drug Gangs Spreading in Colombia," Stratfor.com, 3 April 2002.

76. Dan Molinski, "Colombia Admits That Oil Money Sometimes Ends Up with Rebels," *Wall Street Journal,* 4 February 2003.

77. "The Development Plan Piñata," *El Espectador* (Bogotá), 11 May 2003.

78. "Colombian Soldiers Stole Millions in Drug Money," *Washington Post,* 21 May 2003; "Colombian Army Theft Hampers Reform Efforts," *Financial Times,* 22 May 2003; "Latin America Briefs," *Miami Herald,* 5 November 2003.

79. Alejandro Santos Rubino, "Semana Director on Colombia's Inability to Resolve Social Crisis," *Semana,* 3–9 February 2002.

80. FBIS, "Latin American Defense Chiefs Meet in Brazil," ACANEFE (Panama) 23 April 2003.

81. "Defence Market Latin America," *Armada International,* April/May 2003, pp. 35–48.

82. FBIS, "Brazilian Defense Minister's Views on Role of Armed Forces," *O Estado de São Paolo,* 13 January 2003.

83. FBIS, Valteno de Oliveira, "New Federal Police Chief Says Priority Is to Fight Arms Trafficking," *Brasilia Correio Braziliense,* 2 February 2003.

84. Andrew Sparrow, "Blair 'Will Back Policy of Armed Invasion'?" *Daily Telegraph,* 14 July 2003.

85. Guillermoprieto, "Letter from Colombia: Waiting for War."

86. FBIS, "Brazil to Strengthen Border Security with 13 New Bases," *Madrid EFE,* 4 May 2003.

87. "Lula Proposes Hunger Fund," www.bbc.co.uk.

88. FBIS, Paulo Paiva, "Brazilian Government Applauds Mexico's Postponement of Security Conference," *São Paolo Gazeta Mercantil,* 5 May 2003; "Rebel Recruiting Suspected," *Washington Post,* 22 May 2003.

89. "Brazilian Leader Backs Chavez in Venezuela Crisis," Stratfor.com, 19 December 2002; "Brazil-Argentina Defense Alliance Could Hurt US," ibid., 12 September 2002.

90. John Authers and Sara Silver, "Fox Outlines Goals for Raising Mexico's Profile," *Financial Times,* 27–28 May 2003; "Mexico-Brazil Alignment: Fox's New Foreign Policy Goal," Stratfor.com, 28 May 2003.

91. Kralev, "OAS Balks at Defense Treaty."

92. Michael Kanell, "Shift to Left Tests US-Latin Dealings," *Atlanta Journal-Constitution,* 21 May 2003.

93. FBIS, "Nineteen Rebel Camps Detected in Venezuelan Territory," *Agence France Presse* (Paris), 1 May 2003.

94. Andy Webb-Vidal, "Bogotá and Caracas Tensions at Crisis Point," *Financial Times,* 23 April 2003; "New Drug Gangs Spreading in Colombia," Stratfor.com, 3 April 2002.

95. Robinson, "Terror Close to Home."

96. Cited in "Ecuador: Economic Challenges for the Next President," Stratfor.com, 1 November 2002.

97. Enrique Ghersi, "South America's New Style Military Coup," *Christian Science Monitor,* 19 June 2003; "Bolivia: A Protest Leader's Unspoken Agenda," Stratfor.com, 22 January 2003.

98. Arie Farnan, "Colombia's Civil War Drifts South into Ecuador," *Christian Science Monitor,* 11 August 2002.

99. "FARC, Ecuador and Secret Non-aggression Pacts," Stratfor.com, 15 May 2003.

100. "Ecuador: Account of Arms Trafficking Rejected," *New York Times,* 5 November 2003.

101. "Ecuador Loses More Than $1.2 Billion Annually to Customs Corruption Alone"; "Ecuador Studying Militarization of Customs to Fight Corruption," ACANEFE (Panama), 23 January 2003.

102. Frances Robles, "Leaders of 15 Latin Countries Meeting in a Troubled Peru," *Miami Herald,* 23 May 2003.

103. "Evo Morales: 'No Habrá Alianzas'?" *BBC Mundo.com,* June 27, 2002; "The Violent Effects of Bolivia's Coca Eradication Program," Stratfor.com, 12 April 2002.

104. Novak, "Cultivating Ferment in Bolivia."

105. Ricardo Sandoval, "Mexico Touts Its Intelligence Agency," *Dallas Morning News,* 22 May 2003.

106. de Oliveira, "New Federal Police Chief Says Priority Is to Fight Arms Trafficking."

107. FBIS, Verbitsky, "Argentine Bill to Fight Terrorism."

108. FBIS, "Argentine Army Chief Opposes Military Involvement in Domestic Security Matters."

109. Larry Rohter, "Latin Lands Don't Share Powell's Priorities," *New York Times,* 10 June 2003.

110. "Net Assessment: Latin America—Benign Neglect and Persistent Weakness," Stratfor.com, 16 June 2003.

111. Rubino, "Semana Director on Colombia's Inability to Resolve Social Crisis."

112. Center for Strategic and International Studies (CSIS), "Hemisphere Highlights: Americas Program," CSIS.org, 2, no. 6 (June 2003).

113. Rohter, "Latin Lands Don't Share Powell's Priorities."

114. "Bush Team's Latin America Agenda Mired in the Past," Stratfor.com, 9 September 2002; Patrick Rucker, "Throughout the Americas,

US Increasingly Isolated over Cuba," *Christian Science Monitor,* 12 June 2003.

115. FBIS, "Shining Path Believed to Be Regrouping in Apurimac," *El Correo* (Lima), 2 May 2003; "Peruvian Hostage-taking Raises New Questions about Shining Path," Stratfor.com, 10 June 2003; "Raids Indicate Shining Path's Resurgence," *Chicago Tribune,* 4 July 2003; "World in Brief," *Washington Post,* 10 November 2003.

116. "The FARC, Venezuela and Brazil: Growing Security Concerns in South America," Stratfor.com, 9 April 2003.

117. "New Drug Gangs Spreading in Colombia," Stratfor.com, 3 April 2002.

118. Rowan Scarborough, "Drug Money Sustains Al Qaeda," *Washington Times,* 29 December 2003.

119. Kevin G. Hall, "Peruvian Government Says It Can't Commit to Eliminating Coca," *Miami Herald,* 7 April 2002.

120. FBIS, Vladimir Lopez, "Nicaraguan Foreign Ministry Reacts to OAS Report on Diversion of Weapons," *El Nuevo Diario* (Managua), 21 January 2003; "Nicaraguan Army General Won't Give up All Missiles," *Arizona Daily Star,* 5 November 2003.

121. Warren P. Strobel, "Powell Has Advice on Latin Trip," *Philadelphia Inquirer,* 5 November 2003.

122. Andres Oppenheimer, "New Latin American Poll Spells Trouble for US," *Miami Herald,* 9 November 2003.

123. Jen Ross, "Latin America Eyes Defense Pact," *Washington Times,* 10 February 2004; FBIS, Verbitsky, "Argentine Bill to Fight Terrorism."

CHAPTER TWO

Security Implications of Poor Economic Performance in Latin America
A Framework for Analysis
PAUL D. TAYLOR

In determining the general welfare, conventional wisdom ascribes significant weight to economic performance. Most of us believe that if an economy is doing poorly, bad things will follow. Conversely, it is less likely that a country with a growing and reasonably equitable economy will produce a failed state. When one considers the general optimism about changes in the Americas a decade ago and the pervasive sense of disappointment today, one finds two major factors that may explain the shift. Market-oriented economic models have not registered the important improvements that their proponents had expected, and democracy has not delivered on its promise of a better life for most people.

How Is Security Linked to Economic Performance?

This paper focuses on the first point, addressing questions of how poor economic performance might affect security and the extent to which these consequences are realized in Latin America today. A simple but broad definition of security is posited for this analysis: reasonable freedom from avoidable internal or external threats to a country's territory, citizens, institutions, and interests. The word *avoidable* is intended here to exclude natural disasters.

Different countries have different notions of what degree of freedom from threats is "reasonable." As Bernard Brodie explained,

> Great nations, . . . and especially what we now call the superpowers, will often be concerned with what they deem threats to their security that are often more distant in space, time and even in conception than simply attack upon their home territories. The main reason, of course, is that the superpower feels itself able to do something effective about a threat that remains as yet indirect or remote, which is not true of a small power except in token association with a large power.[1]

Certain ties between security and economics are obvious. Paul Kennedy explained, for example, that "wealth is usually needed to underpin military power and military power is usually needed to acquire and protect wealth."[2]

Several methodological difficulties arise when one tries to relate economic phenomena to their noneconomic consequences. One problem is that the links, even when direct, are often not strong. Frequently, perceptions of economic difficulties have to build psychologically until they reach a critical mass and trigger something else.[3] Thus our ability to predict the effects of economic performance is necessarily more limited than we would like. Moreover, it would be a stretch to ascribe all problems in the security realm to economic performance. When that performance is poor and creates security problems, security may also be harmed by other factors, such as corruption or generally ineffective governance. When possible, I will try to acknowledge those noneconomic influences below. Finally, the topic of this paper requires a demonstration that a causal relationship flows from economic performance to security consequences. Even if this connection pertains, marshaling the evidence may be problematic. Causes by definition need to precede their effects, but the nature of economic data is such that they cannot be measured reliably until some time after the economic performance they are meant to record, by which time the security consequences might already have been felt.

This paper will seek to relate the recent economic performance of several Latin American countries to its impact on security issues. We will not try here to analyze the causes of the economic difficulties themselves.

Theoretical Security Consequences of Poor Economic Performance

Conceptually, one could speculate that disappointing economic performance might impact several factors of security interest:

- Support for democracy could weaken.

- The economic suasions available to criminals and terrorists to undermine security operations could become more potent as the number of people who may be lured by drug traffickers and other criminal organizations and guerilla groups increases in proportion to economic insecurity.

- Militaries and internal security forces could become less capable to address threats and more susceptible to corruption as their resources become more constrained.

- Migration from poorly performing economies could be stimulated.

- Conversely, the war against terrorism could make it more difficult for migrants to remit portions of their earnings back to their countries of origin.

- Governments with sick economies could shift away from policies that encourage growth in trade and investment, thereby reversing the trend toward hemispheric integration. (Inasmuch as the appeals of economic integration have helped overcome bilateral tensions, as in the termination by Argentina and Brazil of their nuclear weapons race as they built the Southern Cone Common Market [MERCOSUR], abandoning economic integration could give rise to renewed tensions among countries of the region.)

- To the extent that disappointing economic results in Latin America were perceived as the consequence of indifferent support by the U.S. government or by international financial institutions, cooperation with the U.S. government on issues across the board, including security, could become more difficult.

With these considerations in mind, the paper will examine the evidence available.

Latin America's Economic Performance

Economic performance encompasses the level of development, the distribution of income, and the state of macroeconomic achievement. Despite gains in per capita income over the past several decades (excepting during the debt crisis of the 1980s), the level of development of the Latin American region remains well below that of countries of the Organization for Economic Cooperation and Development (OECD) and a long way from the level most of its inhabitants would consider satisfactory. Moreover, the distribution of income compares unfavorably with that of all other major geographic regions. Apart from a consideration of income distribution later, this paper will focus on short-term macroeconomic performance and the possible security consequences of downturns. This focus is premised on the belief that changes in *relative* performance are likely to have the most disruptive effects on security.

Regrettably, poor macroeconomic performance in Latin America has been unmistakably clear. Take the cases of the seven largest national economies of Latin America and the Caribbean, countries that account for more than 80 percent of the total population and about 90 percent of the total economic activity of the region. They are Argentina, Brazil, Chile, Colombia, Mexico, Peru, and Venezuela; their economic performance is summarized in table 1. Together they illustrate a pattern of economic performance in the year 2002 that ranged from disastrous, in the cases of Argentina and Venezuela, to lackluster in the other countries except Peru. The effects of weak growth carried disappointing consequences for employment in most countries in the region. High rates of inflation further explained particular discontent in Argentina and Venezuela. Governments' efforts to address their countries' economic difficulties created additional problems. For example, many Argentines saw the sharp devaluation of the Argentine *peso* and the resulting loss in personal savings and investment income as a failure of the state to play by the rules of the game and respect constitutional guarantees.[4]

TABLE 1
*Economic Performance
Percent Changes during 2002*

	GDP	POPULATION	CONSUMER PRICES	VALUE OF CURRENCY
Argentina	-5.2	+1.30	+41.0	-70.3
Brazil	+3.4	+1.21	+12.5	-35.0
Chile	+3.2	+1.26	+2.8	-9.2
Colombia	+2.0	+1.89	+7.0	-20.1
Mexico	+2.3	+1.77	+5.7	-12.1
Peru	+5.2	+1.97	+1.5	-1.7
Venezuela	-16.7	+1.75	+31.2	-45.3

Sources: GDP: *The Economist*, March 29, 2003, and May 24, 2003. Population: data for 1999, Bureau for Latin America and the Caribbean, U.S. Agency for International Development, *2000 Latin America and Caribbean Selected Economic and Social Data.* Consumer Prices: *The Economist*, January 25, 2003. Currency: *The Economist*, January 4, 2003.

Flows of foreign direct investment (FDI) to Latin America and the Caribbean plunged by one-third in 2002, to $56.7 billion from $84 billion in 2001. This decline compared with a drop of 12.6 percent in 2000, and another 11 percent in 2001.[5] The drop in FDI was a response to slower economic growth in the region and, in turn, exacerbated that trend by reducing the prospects for an early recovery.

This disappointing short-term performance early in the first decade of the twenty-first century occurred in the context of an already-disconcerting level of economic insecurity in Latin America and the Caribbean. Dani Rodrik, in a paper published in 1999, cited surveys undertaken in the region:

> A large cross-national survey of 14 Latin American countries recently found that 61 percent of the respondents thought that their parents had lived better than they do. Moreover, less than half of the respondents (46 percent) thought that their children would end up having better lives than themselves, with that percentage varying from as little as 30 percent in Mexico to 61 percent in Chile.

> The same survey identified a strong demand for social insurance in the region. Almost three-quarters of the respondents favored increased spending on unemployment insurance, and more than 80 percent expressed a desire for more spending on pensions.[6]

Latin America Compared with the World

A major contributor to poor economic performance in Latin America was the desultory pace of economic activity in the major world economies. Growth in GDP in the OECD region, estimated at only 2.6 percent in 2002, ended on a gloomy note, with growth in the fourth quarter turning down to 0.4 percent compared with 0.8 percent in the third quarter.[7] With about half of Latin America's total exports going to the United States and accounting for some $200 billion annually in foreign exchange earnings for the region, the importance of the rate of U.S. growth is evident. The U.S. economy showed signs of strong recovery late in 2003, but the performance of the economies of the European Union and Japan continued to lag.

As early as 6 September 2003 one important manifestation of these trends could be seen in the downturn in FDI; on that date *The Economist* reported that after impressive growth year after year from 1991 to 2000, the level of FDI dropped in 2001 and again in 2002, reaching only about $650 billion in 2002, compared with more than $1.35 trillion in the year 2000. Annual declines of 71 percent in North America and 41 percent in Africa greatly surpassed the drop of 33 percent from 2001 to 2002 registered in Latin America and the Caribbean.

Latin American presidents and finance ministers could take comfort in the realization that economic performance in some other parts of the world was even worse than in their countries, and also in the understanding that some of their countries' problems were a result of forces beyond their control. Most of their citizens, though, were more likely to measure their own economic well-being against what it used to be or against what they expected it to be than to compare it to that of another place. It is not easy for most people to weigh their current economic situation against that of an abstract person in another country.

Support for Democracy

We start with a question: does poor economic performance undermine support for democracy?

One may also wonder why democracy is a security issue. One simple answer is that the United States has chosen to make it so by stressing in Latin America a policy agenda predicated on four complementary goals:

- The promotion of democracy

- The encouragement of responsible government

- The strengthening of security

- The stimulation of economic development.

Paula J. Dobriansky, undersecretary of state for global affairs, stressed before the Association of American Chambers of Commerce in Latin America that "these goals all relate to and reinforce one another." She added, "The foundation of prosperity and stability is a democratic system of government."[8]

This conviction is widely shared by other governments of the Western Hemisphere. The Inter-American Democratic Charter adopted by members of the Organization of American States (OAS) in September 2001 represented a consensus among all member states on the concept that a threat to one democracy in the hemisphere is a threat to all. Not coincidentally, this formulation echoed the language that the Rio Treaty applied to threats against the territory of a member state.

The history of the last two decades in Latin America has been one of political transformation from authoritarian regimes in most countries to democratically elected governments, and of economic transformation from statist, inward-looking economies to more open, market-oriented economies following the neoliberal model of the Washington Consensus.[9] It would not be surprising if citizens, unhappy that they have not felt a marked improvement in their sense of well-being, found it difficult to determine whether it was the economic or the political reforms that had failed them.

The available evidence suggests that while Latin American economies languished, most Latin American citizens became less supportive of democracy from 2002 to 2003. This was the conclusion of opinion polls conducted by Latinobarometro.[10] Support for democracy continued to decline from 1997 levels after an uptick in 2002.

Secretary of State Colin L. Powell recognized before the OAS that, "Our citizens know that free and fair elections alone do not guarantee effective, accountable government. . . . New democracies created with high hopes can founder if the lives of ordinary citizens do not change for the better."[11] In the language of the 2003 Policy Report of the Inter-American Dialogue, "Democracy in Latin America is unlikely to thrive while economic growth is anemic, unemployment is at record levels, poverty and steep inequality are pervasive, and most people believe their lives will be worse than those of their parents."[12]

A logical question in this regard is why the region has not seen a resurgence in recent years of the coups that led to a preponderance of military governments in Latin America during the 1960s and 1970s. One may find an explanation in the changed external environment, evolution in the aspirations of military leaders in the region, and democratic maturation on the part of Latin American publics.

The collapse of the Soviet Union greatly altered the context in which both Washington and Latin American governments operate. When the Cold War was raging and a robust Soviet/Cuban apparatus was poised to exploit opportunities to expand its influence in the Western Hemisphere, successive U.S. governments and Latin American militaries easily achieved consensus on the need to unite against a shared security threat. When the question came down to a choice between protecting democracy or countering a threat to security, security considerations usually trumped. The tide began to turn during the 1980s, when democracy came to be perceived more as a bulwark against Soviet influence than as a rival of security. For the United States, the centerpiece of this policy

FIGURE 1
Latin American Opinions of Democracy

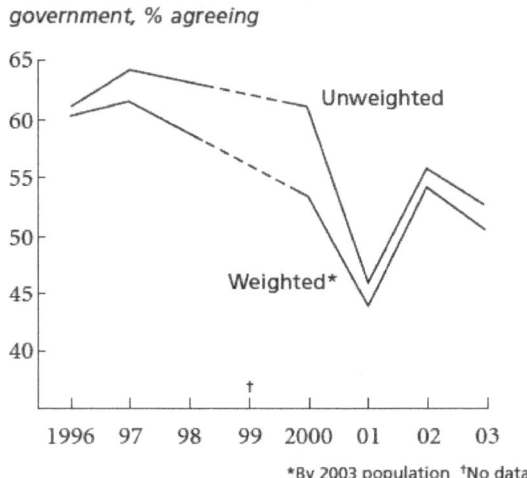

Democracy is preferable to any other kind of government, % agreeing

Unweighted

Weighted*

1996 97 98 99 2000 01 02 03

*By 2003 population †No data

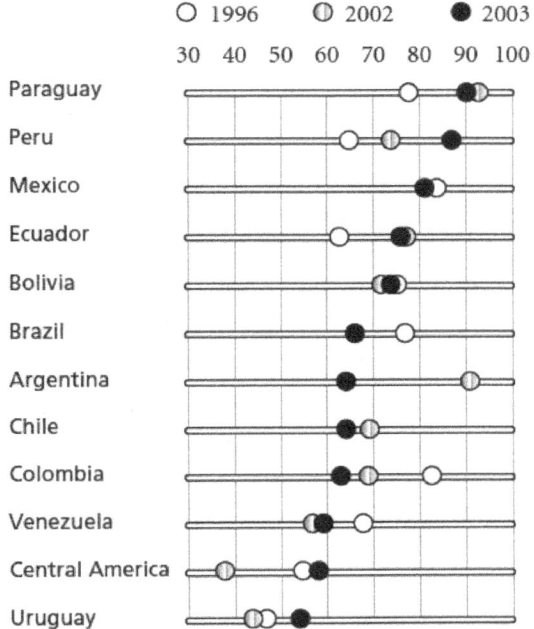

How satisfied are you with the way democracy works in your country? % responding "not very satisfied" and "not at all satisfied"

○ 1996   ◐ 2002   ● 2003

30 40 50 60 70 80 90 100

Paraguay
Peru
Mexico
Ecuador
Bolivia
Brazil
Argentina
Chile
Colombia
Venezuela
Central America
Uruguay

Sources: Latinobarómetro; EIU. *The Economist,* 1 November 2003. By permission.

was, of course, support for elected government in El Salvador against the armed insurgency supported by an authoritarian Nicaraguan regime allied with Cuba and the Soviet Union. This emphasis was complemented by a push in U.S. policy against the dictatorships in Chile and Paraguay and support for transitions to democracy elsewhere in the hemisphere.

Simultaneously, the Latin American debt crisis and the severe economic contraction that was forced on most countries in the region provided a powerful incentive for those military officers who had assumed political power to return to their barracks. It was with some sense of relief that, between 1981 and 1991, they handed the reins of government over to elected civilians in all of the countries of South and Central America, except Colombia, Costa Rica, Ecuador, and Venezuela, which already had elected governments at the beginning of the period. While they may have had reasons to want to hang on to political power, military officers found little joy in exercising responsibility after the debt crisis had denied their countries access to the financing traditionally available from international lenders. For their part, Latin American publics were happy to be rid of people and policies that had failed to deliver acceptable economic results. The new governments were fragile, to say the least, in most countries, so they welcomed international support for democracy. This support built steadily on a bilateral basis throughout the late 1980s and 1990s until it was formally embodied multilaterally in the Inter-American Democratic Charter, adopted on 11 September 2001.

Latin American publics themselves also underwent an impressive democratic maturation. The severe economic crises of recent years in Argentina and Venezuela have not prompted widespread calls for military government. The number of those positively answering a question from pollsters of whether "democracy is preferable to any other kind of government" did drop somewhat—from 71 percent to 65 percent—in Argentina from 1996 to 2002 but recovered to 68 percent in 2003, probably reflecting both the beginning of a recovery from the economic collapse of 2001 and the popularity of the new president, Néstor Kirchner. In Venezuela, pro-democratic responses actually increased from 62 to 75 percent by 2002 before dropping to 67 percent in 2003.[13] This sentiment could be seen in the reversal of the attempt to oust President Chávez in 2002.

Instead of jettisoning the democratic form of government, voters in several countries demonstrated a sophisticated ability to place blame on the policies, and sometimes the persons, they held responsible for disappointing performance. Clearly a common denominator in the elections of Hugo Chávez in Venezuela, Luiz Inácio Lula da Silva in Brazil, Lucio Gutiérrez in Ecuador, and Néstor Kirchner in Argentina was dissatisfaction with their countries' economic performance. In the cases of Chávez and Gutiérrez, corruption in the governments they replaced was also an important factor. It is hard to weigh the strength of people's economic disappointment against abhorrence of corruption in motivating their votes, but the voters have largely chosen to focus on personalities and policies rather than to turn, as in the past, to the military institution for political salvation. Part of the appeal of Chávez and Gutiérrez surely stemmed from their images as strong individuals who had come to prominence as army officers in coup attempts. Describing Gutiérrez, Andrés Benavente Urbina wrote, "Emulating Chávez, he presented himself dressed in a green military jacket that evoked his military past and symbolized an authoritarian image for his eventual performance as political leader."[14] Nevertheless, Chávez and Gutiérrez derived their presidential power from the ballot box rather than from a tank turret.

Proponents of democracy can be heartened, instead of discouraged, by electoral processes that change the course of public policy. The ability to alter policy is a prerequisite for political accountability and a hopeful sign of political maturation in the hemisphere. The widening realization that a leader can favor shifting the rewards of public policy to less advantaged segments of society without having the process exploited from abroad is but the latest benefit of the end of the Cold War. From the perspective of the United States, favoring democratic and reformist government is far less likely to conflict with its security objective than it might have been a generation ago.

If Chávez, da Silva, Gutiérrez, and Kirchner got elected in part because their promise to effect some shift in economic policy was seen as an antidote to disappointments associated with the neoliberal model, the pressure will be on them to succeed with new economic policies. So far, their commitment to new policies has gone largely unrealized. The economic mandates of da Silva and Gutiérrez were somewhat blurred by their embrace late in their presidential campaigns of such tenets of the Washington Consensus as cooperation with foreign lenders and receptivity to foreign investment. Chávez has made less headway in reforming Venezuela's economic structure than he has in implementing his own brand of political reform.

Nevertheless, if these leaders cannot deliver a better standard of living to their populations, interest in nondemocratic approaches to governance could be fueled. In other words, democratic elections have enabled a potentially important policy shift; but the jury is still out on whether the new leaders' policies will be significantly different, or whether continued economic failure might raise doubts about the democratic model itself after alternative policy agendas have been tried. So far both da Silva and Gutiérrez have decided to work with international financiers, both official and commercial lenders. If their approach bears fruit, it may contribute to a strengthening of support for democracy. If not, their departure from the more statist platforms on which they were elected could cause some supporters to conclude that democracy itself had failed them.

Recent declines in support for democracy track economic declines in many Latin American countries, but not all. The cases of Venezuela and Argentina, with serious economic difficulties in 2001 and 2002, suggest that the correlation may sometimes even be inverse. While there has been a general weakening of public support for democracy throughout Latin America during the past half decade, economic performance during that period has been mixed. Concern over problems of governance, such as corruption and other crime, may have been important factors in shaping public perceptions of democracy.

Internal Security

One could expect poor economic performance to worsen internal security in at least two ways. Economic hardship could cause some people to turn to crime as a means of support while making others more vulnerable to subornation by well-financed drug dealers or terrorists. At the same time, economic difficulties might strain government budgets and reduce the resources available for security forces.

Colombia

The government of Colombia incurs costs on several fronts as it addresses the longest-lasting and most violent security challenge in the hemisphere—that is, the sustained campaign by allied narcotics and terrorist enterprises. The government recognizes, in the language of Richard Millet, that while "there is no military solution to the Colombian crisis, it is also true that there is no solution without a meaningful military component."[15] Seeking improved security as his top priority, President Alvaro Uribe plans to raise defense spending (including that for police and pensions) from 3.5 percent of GDP to 5.8 percent by the end of his term in 2006.[16] His government knows that success in the war depends also on giving rural populations hope for the future and alternatives to employment in cultivating and processing narcotics. Rural development is expensive, but experts in counterinsurgency see it as a requirement for winning the hearts and minds of rural populations.[17] One indicator of the enormity of this task is the daunting challenge of providing livelihoods for the estimated six hundred thousand Colombians employed in the drug trade if Plan Colombia succeeds in destroying the narcotics industry.

The attacks by terrorists on major pipelines and petroleum processing facilities have complicated the challenge for the government to meet a commitment under Plan Colombia to provide five billion dollars as its share of the program.[18] The immediately adverse impact of these attacks on the Colombian economy is exacerbated by their longer-term impact in discouraging foreign investment in the country. The two-way relationship between security and economic performance is clear in the Colombian case. A strong economy is needed to pay for the security and development programs that are essential to address the security threat; the most serious impediment to stronger investment and more robust growth is investors' lack of confidence in the security situation. The U.S. Andean Counterdrug Initiative attempts to help Colombia break out of this vicious economic-security cycle by providing $731 million for "social and economic development as well as for counternarcotics and security efforts."[19]

The case of Colombia demonstrates that an economy can be both a target of terrorists and an essential element in their defeat; major security and developmental expenditures may have to be funded, either from domestic sources or foreign assistance.

Argentina

The Argentine case is more clearly one in which serious economic problems developed and predated other important domestic political and social problems. When President Adolfo Rodriguez Saa declared a moratorium on his country's $155 billion public debt on 23 December 2001, he did far more than effect the largest such default by any country in history.[20] One of the first consequences was his own prompt resignation. Within a year, 60 percent of the country's thirty-seven million people—double the number at the end of 2001—had slipped below the poverty level, defined as an income of less than $220 a month for a family of four.[21] Many Argentines, facing freezes on their savings accounts, tight controls on foreign exchange transactions, shortages of imported goods ranging from Chilean salmon to critical medicines, sharply inflated prices, and unemployment, took to the streets to attack banks and politicians. Crime soared, and the rate of Argentine deaths attributed to criminal violence surpassed the level in war-torn Colombia.[22] Increasing needs for help with social problems were met by a decline in social services caused by the budgetary crisis that the economic collapse had triggered.

Some two and a half years after the economic crisis had come to a head, there were indications that an end was in sight. A new president, Néstor Kirchner, took office on 25 May 2003. Although the strength of his mandate was limited by the decision of former president Carlos Menem to withdraw from a runoff election, and even though Kirchner's previous experience in government was limited to provincial politics, the Argentine public seemed hopeful that he could succeed. This sentiment could become a self-fulfilling prophecy. In June 2003, Kirchner's government reached a long-delayed accord with the International Monetary Fund to begin negotiations on a multiyear agreement that promised essential relief.

Brazil

Brazil offers a different case. Luis Bitencourt, in his study, conducted for the Americas Program of the Center for Strategic and International Studies (CSIS), on Brazil's grow-ing urban insecurity, notes that during the last ten years crime statistics for cities such as Rio de Janeiro, São Paolo, Espírito Santo, and Recife have skyrocketed.[23] He asserts that the populations of these cities are frightened and skeptical about the state's ability to protect them, and he judges that "the situation is so grave that in some urban regions criminal gangs command more obedience than the authority of the state." Bitencourt documents a doubling in the murder rate per capita between 1979 and 1997.

Bitencourt includes among the causes of the deterioration of urban public safety "pov-erty, and especially the huge gap existing between the rich and the poor [which] creates a fertile environment where drug dealers circulate and establish areas of influence."[24] For Bitencourt, however, the economic aspect is but one of many factors causing secu-rity to deteriorate. Inefficiencies in law enforcement and the judicial system, gaps and overlaps in the federal system, and failures in intelligence all contribute.

The problem of deteriorating urban public safety has been getting worse for years, in good economic times and bad. While economic difficulties may have contributed to this trend, it is equally clear that other factors were at play that could by themselves have explained the decline in urban security.

Venezuela

The Venezuelan situation has elements of economic distress and violence. The relation-ship between them may be unique. As noted above, Venezuela's GDP fell more than 16 percent in 2002, and unemployment approached 20 percent, with thousands of busi-nesses closing and capital flight amounting to billions of dollars.[25] More than elsewhere in the region, Venezuela became polarized politically, with the government blaming the poor economy on, first, decades of official neglect of the poor and, recently, a series of prolonged national strikes organized by the political opposition to try to cripple and eventually topple the government. The opposition blamed the poor economy on gov-ernmental mismanagement.

President Chávez's creation of Bolivarian Circles—loosely organized groups of his most ardent followers—deepened the polarization and contributed to violence and a pattern of intimidation of opponents to the government. Although definitive information was elusive about the numbers of adherents, their training, and the extent to which they are armed, the Bolivarian Circles and the reaction they have induced have undoubtedly been responsible for increased unrest.[26]

Many disgruntled Venezuelans cited the poor performance of the Venezuelan economy under the Chávez government as a principal grievance, and some may have been driven to civic violence by economic factors alone. A more compelling explanation of violence, though, was the sense in both the government and its opposition that the other side lacked legitimacy and was intent on effecting changes that would deny citizens their basic rights. The opposition complained that Chávez was antidemocratic, governed in a chaotic and confrontational way, and was too influenced by Fidel Castro.[27] The government and its supporters argued that previous governments and the traditional Venezuelan establishment had been blithely indifferent to the needs of the poor. Nearly 40 percent of the population remained loyal to the government even as petitioners demanded a recall vote.[28] Under these circumstances, both sides resorted to violence to further their political agendas, in which economic issues were but one factor.

Bolivia

Recent events in Bolivia bear mention even though Bolivia is not among the seven largest economies on which this paper is primarily focused. These events demonstrate connections among economic performance, crime, and political instability. Bolivia suffers from the lowest per capita income among the countries of South America, one of the least equitable distributions of income in Latin America, and a pattern of growth that has stalled for the past five years.

This situation provided an ideal setting for the cultivation of illicit narcotics and the political mobilization at which Evo Morales has been so successful. As a leader of the coca growers' federation and a member of Congress, Morales has been able to forge links among the economically disadvantaged, indigenous citizens who feel aggrieved by the pattern of Caucasian domination of Bolivia's political life, and those who believe that the benefits of international transactions usually accrue to foreigners or to a few privileged Bolivians. Marta Lagos, a Chilean political analyst whose firm, Latino-barómetro, has done surveys of public opinion in Bolivia, observed that "Bolivians are suspicious of whoever is making the deal because they think, 'The elite always puts money in its own pockets, and we are left on the streets with nothing to eat.'"[29]

Morales came within two percentage points of defeating Gonzalo Sánchez de Losada in the 2002 presidential election. With just over 22 percent of the vote, Sánchez won a decision in Congress that paved the way for a second presidential term, which he commenced amidst widespread resentment over his government's embrace of economic policies urged on it by the United States, the World Bank, and the International Monetary Fund. With jobs scarce in Bolivia, emigration to neighboring Argentina and Chile accelerated over the past decade.[30] Sánchez pursued a U.S.-backed campaign to eradicate coca production without obtaining adequate funding to couple it with his "alternative development" program to encourage farmers to grow crops like pineapples, bananas, coffee, black pepper, oregano, and passion fruit on land once devoted to coca.[31]

This confluence of forces provided the context in which the government's proposal to export natural gas to Mexico and the United States via a port in Chile—Bolivia's long-standing enemy—was received. Eduardo Gamarra, a Bolivian scholar who directs the Center for Latin American and Caribbean Studies at Florida International University, commented that "Evo Morales and others have shrewdly used [the Free Trade Area of the Americas or the gas export law] as a flag which plays on [people's] deepest fears, the loss of identity and the giving away of what they consider to be their national patrimony."[32]

Well-organized protests aimed immediately at the proposal to export natural gas resulted in the deaths of more than eighty protesters and led to the resignation of President Sánchez de Losada on 17 October 2003. Poverty was a reason farmers were attracted to coca cultivation, and economic constraints had made the government's program for its eradication less likely to succeed. The strong sense of economic injustice that Evo Morales and others were able to exploit in racial terms added weight to the argument that governmental policy lacked legitimacy because it corruptly benefited ethnic and economic elites.

Privatization and Corruption

Other examples of economic phenomena creating public disorder were provided when violent protests in mid-2002 caused both Peru and Paraguay to abandon plans to privatize public firms. In Peru, protestors expressed fear that privatization would create unjustified windfalls for the politically well connected as well as higher utility tariffs and job losses.[33] For many citizens, corruption in public life and their own unsatisfactory economic plight are two sides of the same coin.

Public intolerance for further sacrifice and a lack of faith in economic reforms, absent a perceptible shift in the distribution of political power, serve as serious constraints on the ability of many governments to carry out the secondary reforms needed to consolidate effective democratic governance—reforms such as improving systems of taxation and administration of justice. A recent Latin American poll cited by the Inter-American Development Bank (IDB) noted that 63 percent of the respondents thought the result of privatization of state enterprises was negative. One of the report's authors, Eduardo Lora, principal economist of the research department of the IDB, commented, "What makes Latin Americans frustrated are not the privatizations themselves but the corruption that surrounds them."[34]

Polling by Latinobarómetro found that support for the privatization of state companies was outweighed by opposition to privatization and had dropped significantly from 1998 to 2003.

Fourteen out of twenty-one Latin American and Caribbean countries included in the latest Corruption Perceptions Index, prepared by Transparency International from multiple sources, fall into the more corrupt half of the 102 countries covered. Only Chile (in seventeenth place) and Uruguay (in thirty-second) qualify for the top third— that is, among the least corrupt countries. Seven Latin American countries are among the worst 20 percent surveyed.[35] The pervasive corruption in most countries of the region has negative consequences for both democracy and development. As it weakens faith in the legitimacy and equity of government, corruption also dampens investment by firms and individuals who have a range of choices when deciding where to place their resources.[36] Furthermore, corruption is facilitated when crime is high and governmental resources are sparse, providing havens for illegal criminal and nonstate actors who threaten U.S. interests.

Migratory Pressures and Remittances

Most contemporary immigration is economically driven, a consequence of differences in employment opportunities between sending and receiving countries.[37] In the Western Hemisphere, some of the migration from Cuba and Colombia is also motivated by political and security factors. Because economic differentials are the principal driver of migration in the Americas, one would expect poor economic performance in the short term to spur migration. Regrettably, the data are not available to permit an examination of whether the recent downturn stimulated an increase in migratory flows. This question merits further research.

Several security implications of known migratory patterns are worth noting. Twenty million people of Latin American and Caribbean origin live outside their own countries. Seven out of ten of these reside in the United States, legally or otherwise.[38] People from Latin America and the Caribbean make up 52.2 percent of the foreign-born population in the United States, and two-thirds of these come from Mexico and Central America.[39] Interestingly in terms of the present analysis, recent migration within Latin America has fallen; this decline is associated in part with the reduction in opportunities for employment in the main traditional destination countries, Argentina and Venezuela.[40]

Most immigrants from Latin America to the United States are men with low-level skills but average educational levels higher than those of their countries of origin.[41] Among immigrants from South America and the Caribbean, however, people with medium to high-level skills are the most common. In fact, economic troubles in Argentina caused an exodus of highly educated professionals.[42] Overall, the immigrants help to alleviate labor shortages in the recipient countries but constitute a loss of human capital for their countries of origin. The drain of educated citizens can contribute to deterioration in a sending country's capacity to produce goods and services, with negative repercussions for terms of trade, productivity, and competitiveness.[43] Migration may, though, provide a political benefit to sending countries, as it creates an escape valve for the discontent of unemployed or underemployed people. Recent flows of migrants from economically stressed countries of Latin America have not produced serious frictions with native populations in receiving countries.

A potentially serious security problem for recipient countries may stem from undocumented immigration. Using a combination of demographic and statistical procedures, the Economic Commission for Latin America and the Caribbean estimated that in 1996 there were some five million undocumented immigrants in the United States. Most of these had entered "without inspection"; the remainder had overstayed their visas.[44] Together they demonstrated the porosity of the U.S. border, the existence of widespread and effective "coyote" networks that facilitate illegal immigration, and the inability of authorities to identify and expel undocumented immigrants. These realities offer opportunities to international terrorist networks interested in inserting operatives into the United States to attack targets there.

Heightened concern about this possibility after 11 September 2001 dashed Mexican president Vicente Fox's hopes for major immigration reform and dampened U.S.-Mexican goodwill for more than two years. The initiatives on immigration that President George W. Bush proposed early in 2004 represented a thaw that could, if implemented, alter U.S.-Mexican relations.

It remains to be seen whether the increasing awareness of the links between immigration and security will lead to a willingness to take stronger measures to force employers to check workers' credentials.[45] Though most employers who depend on illegal immigrants do not like to talk about it, their eagerness to employ such workers is a reality. The International Organization for Migration observed that "among advanced industrialized countries, the United States has the toughest penalties for immigrant smuggling and related activities, yet is amongst the lowest in terms of penalties against employers."[46] The influence of employers competes politically with the concerns of citizens who may feel uncomfortable about the presence of millions of undocumented foreigners.

Meanwhile, immigrants from Latin America, documented or not, have contributed mightily to better the economic situations in their home countries by remitting an estimated $25 billion a year (in the year 2002), an amount well in excess of total official development assistance to those countries and, for many of the smaller economies, equivalent to a significant share of their export earnings.[47]

TABLE 2

*Latin America and the Caribbean: Main Countries Receiving Remittances
1990 and 2000*

	MILLIONS OF DOLLARS		AVERAGE ANNUAL VARIATION	% OF GDP		% OF EXPORTS	
	1990	2000	1990–2000 (%)	1990	2000	1990	2000
Latin America and the Caribbean	**4,766**	**17,334**	**13.8**	**0.4**	**0.9**	**2.7**	**4.2**
Mexico	2,492	6,573	10.2	0.9	1.1	5.1	3.6
El Salvador	357	1,751	17.2	7.9	13.6	36.7	47.8
Dominican Republic	315	1,689	18.3	4.5	8.5	17.2	18.8
Colombia	488	1,118	8.6	1.2	1.3	5.6	7.2
Brazil	527	1,113	7.8	0.1	0.2	1.5	1.7
Ecuador	50	1,084[a]	36.0	0.5	8.0	1.5	18.7
Jamaica	136	789	19.2	3.2	10.8	6.1	23.3[b]
Cuba	—	720	—	—	2.5	—	15.0
Peru	87	718	23.5	0.2	1.3	2.1	8.4
Guatemala	107	563	18.1	1.4	3.0	6.8	14.9
Honduras	50	410	23.4	1.6	6.9	4.8	16.3
Nicaragua	10[c]	320	41.4	0.9	13.4	2.6	34.0
Other	147	487	12.7	0.1	0.1	0.2	0.4

Notes:
a. Figure for 1999.
b. Figure for 1998.
c. Figure for 1992.

Sources: ECLAC, on the basis of figures from the International Monetary Fund (IMF), *Balance of Payments Statistics. 2001 Year-
book,* Washington, D.C., 2001; Cuba: estimates by the country. Cited in ECLAC, *Globalization and Development,* p. 247. Only
the inflows or remittances by the country in question are taken into account.

These remittances move with little interference from U.S. authorities, who are anxious
to retain the unfettered pattern of capital flows into and out of U.S. markets. This
treatment could have been altered by increased concern about security considerations
in the war on terrorism. There was a possibility that controls would be imposed on remittances to deny financing of international terrorist groups from the United States.
This possibility has been reduced, however, by authorities' success in imposing selective
controls to keep funds from flowing to narco-terrorist groups in Colombia or to Arab
groups, operating in the Triple Frontier region of Argentina, Brazil, and Paraguay, that
channeled charitable contributions to terrorist causes.

Recent migration from countries in economic distress removed a potential source of
political disruption without creating unmanageable disruption in receiving countries,
which often benefited from the infusion of labor. These results of migration enhanced
overall security. Remittances by migrants have had a significant positive economic impact on their countries of origin, but the benefits have been very unevenly distributed
among the countries of Latin America and the Caribbean.

Worse Relations between Latin America and the United States

As the biggest economic player in the Western Hemisphere, the largest trading partner, and a major actor in international financial institutions, the United States is the country to which many Latin Americans look when they seek someone to blame for their troubles. Sometimes Washington makes it easy to fault the U.S. government, as when former treasury secretary Paul O'Neill articulated a prescription of "tough love" for Argentina so bluntly that he seemed almost to revel in it. When Washington underscores its words with unfriendly actions, such as imposing supplemental tariffs on steel goods or a farm bill laced with domestic supports and export subsidies that have the effect of depressing the incomes of farmers in Latin America, it invites criticism from its neighbors.

Obviously, the positions of Chile and Mexico on a resolution in the United Nations Security Council to authorize the use of force in Iraq—a major U.S. security priority— were viewed as unhelpful by the United States. They may have been popular at home because of a perception of U.S. indifference to Latin American problems. Ironically, the discord emerged just after Chile had negotiated a free trade agreement with the United States and at a time when Mexico had the closest economic relations with the United States of any Latin American country. A consequence of close trading relations is trade disputes, as the United States has experienced with Canada and the European Union. In fact, the difficulties of Mexican farmers in adjusting to the phase-in of liberalized treatment for agricultural goods under the North American Free Trade Agreement may have strained relations just as the UN vote was being considered. President Fox's disappointment over the failure to win a liberalization of U.S. immigration practices was another factor.

Latin Americans' perceptions of the United States have been turning more negative. According to polling by Latinobarómetro, in 2000, 67 percent of respondents in Mexico and South America held a "good" or "very good" opinion of the United States. By 2003, those responses had fallen to 53 percent, while 39 percent admitted to a "bad" or "very bad" opinion, up from 18 percent in 2000.[48]

The enthusiastically cordial reception Fidel Castro received when he visited Buenos Aires in May 2003 may have related to his image of defiance of the United States, capitalism, and the international financial status quo. That event by itself lacked real security significance, but it contributed to worsening the context in which governments have to decide important things.

The eagerness of the United States to back assistance to Brazil and Uruguay in August 2002 stood in contrast to its prior stance vis-à-vis Argentina. The situations were different with respect to some elements of economic policy; and Brazil's economy was

FIGURE 2
Latin American Opinions of the United States

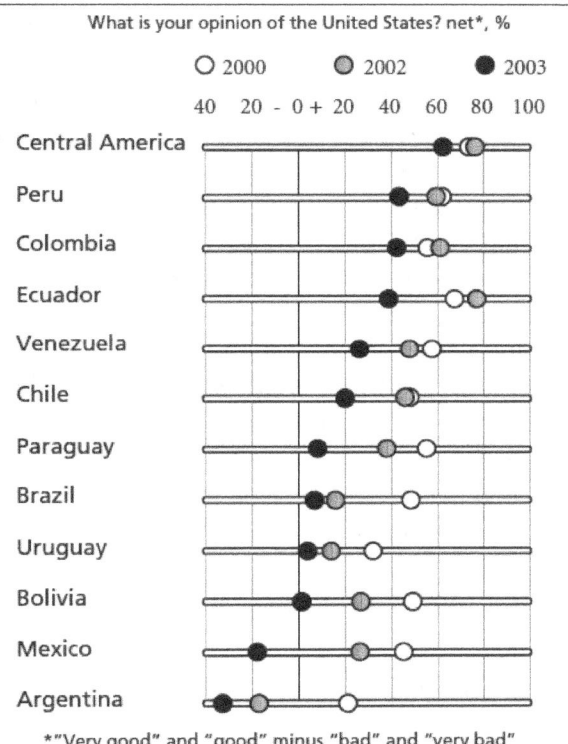

What is your opinion of the United States? net*, %

○ 2000   ◐ 2002   ● 2003

40   20 - 0 + 20   40   60   80   100

Central America
Peru
Colombia
Ecuador
Venezuela
Chile
Paraguay
Brazil
Uruguay
Bolivia
Mexico
Argentina

*"Very good" and "good" minus "bad" and "very bad"

Source: The Economist, 1 November 2003. By permission.

much larger than Argentina's, so the potential of its collapse was far more threatening to the international financial system. Nevertheless, the strong support Washington provided for the International Monetary Fund's $30 billion rescue package can be seen in part as an admission that the U.S. posture on Argentina's financial plight had been too strident. Further interaction with the government of Luiz Inácio Lula da Silva, especially Washington's unwavering determination to accent the positive and ignore philosophical differences, indicates that it may have taken to heart charges that its criticism of Hugo Chávez and open support of his opponents contributed to a perception that the United States was not foursquare in favor of democratic governance in the Americas.[49]

Substantive economic relations between the United States and Latin American economies actually served to ameliorate the economic downturn in Latin America. Patterns of trade between the United States and Latin America adjusted to the slowdown in growth in Latin America and generally stronger rates of economic activity in the

United States (see figure 3). Since the year 2000, U.S. exports to Latin America have declined from a record $171 billion to $149 billion in 2002, while imports dropped only
$5 billion—from $209 billion to $204 billion. The result was a significant increase in
the U.S. trade deficit with the region, which had grown from $5 billion in 1997 to $39
billion in 2000, and to $55 billion in 2002.

As by far the largest foreign market for Latin American producers, the U.S. economy
offset some of the downturn that otherwise would have created even greater levels of
unemployed capacity in their home markets. The commercial relationships among literally millions of traders throughout the hemisphere strengthened nongovernmental
bonds that continued to draw the United States and its neighbors closer. In contrast,
though, to foreign direct investment, which had been in decline since 2000, nearly all
of the trade decisions took place exclusively in the private sector, without any explicit
governmental involvement. While FDI decisions are often private, sometimes major
decisions on where to build a new factory or whether to buy a foreign company become the objects of high-level attention in the governments of the parties to a potential
transaction. In these cases, governments' eagerness to have their firms succeed may
make them more cooperative in other aspects of foreign relations.

In contrast to the days when dependency theory dominated intellectual appreciations
of international economic relations and many countries of Latin America were

FIGURE 3
U.S. Trade with Latin America

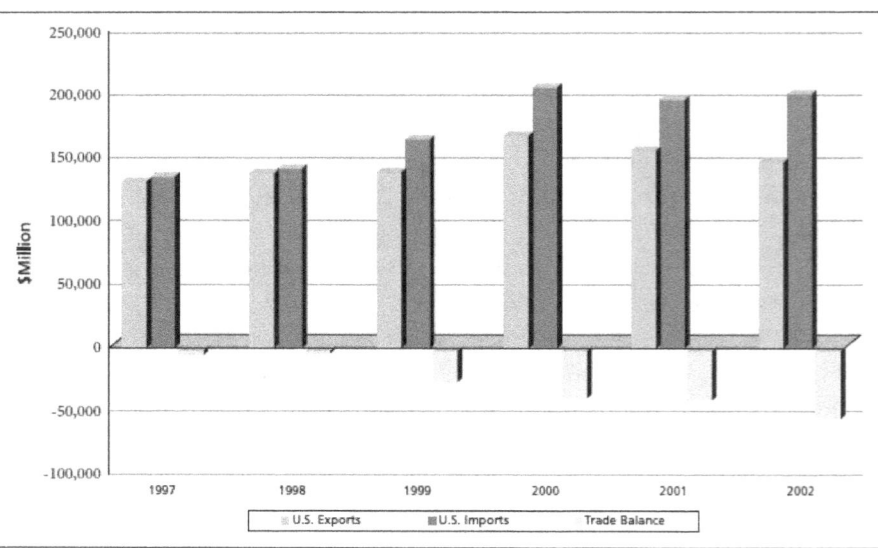

Source: U.S. Census Bureau, *U.S. Trade Balance with Latin America (Excluding Mexico)* and *Trade Balance with Mexico*, available at
www.census.gov/foreign-trade/balance/c2010.html.

governed by authoritarian regimes backed by the United States, current blame of the United States may be mild. Whatever the U.S. stance on economic issues, though, a perception that the war on terrorism has diverted the attention of the United States to other regions may make it harder for Washington to win support on its security agenda, especially when the threat to countries in Latin America is seen as weak, as in the case of Iraq. Just as in NATO Europe, achieving a shared perception of a threat is necessary to convincing other countries to accept any sacrifice to meet it.

Will Latin America's Economic Performance Ever Be Satisfactory? The Challenge of Income Distribution

Latin America and the Caribbean hold the dubious honor of possessing the least equitable distribution of income of any region in the world. The Inter-American Development Bank described the situation in the region this way:

> A quarter of all national income is received by a mere 5 percent of the population, and the top 10 percent receive 40 percent. Such proportions are comparable only to those found in some individual African countries, whose per capita income levels are half those of Latin America, and they are considerably higher than those of any other group of countries. In Southeast Asian countries, the wealthiest 5 percent receive 16 percent of all national income on average, while in the developed countries they receive 13 percent.

> The counterpoint to the great concentration of income in the hands of wealthy Latin Americans is found at the other end of the income scale in Latin America: the poorest 30 percent of the population receive only 7.5 percent of total income, less than any [other region of] the world.[50]

Several implications for security flow from this distribution of income. First, there is an inverse association between concentration of income and acceptance of democracy. There is also a strong relationship between the distribution of income and rates of poverty. Additionally, poor distribution of income fuels migration. Finally, income inequality, as well as poor economic performance, has an impact on crime rates.

Public opinion polling shows a clear relationship between a country's income distribution and the degree of support for democracy there (see figure 4).[51] Where income inequality is less pronounced, as in Uruguay or Costa Rica, a high proportion of the population believes that "democracy is preferable to any other kind of government." In the more unequal countries, there is a greater tendency to accept authoritarian governments and more people think that "it makes no difference whether a regime is democratic or nondemocratic."[52]

More than a third of Latin Americans live at the poverty level, under two dollars a day—the minimum considered necessary to cover basic consumption needs. In its report on inequality, the Inter-American Development Bank calculated that if Latin American countries had the income distribution typically found in other countries at a similar level of development, the incidence of poverty would be half what it actually

FIGURE 4

Income Concentration and Acceptance of Democracy

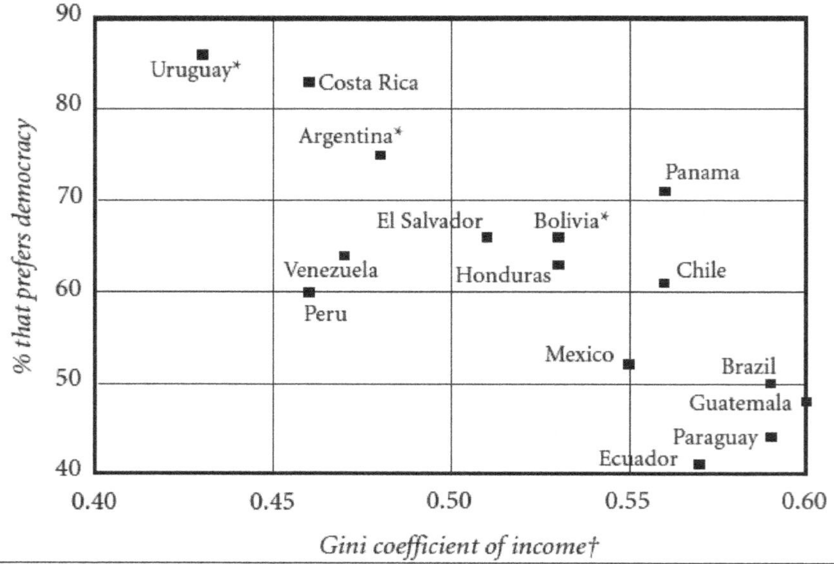

Source: Latinobarómetro and IDB calculations based on recent household surveys.

* Countries with urban data only.

† The Gini coefficient indicates the relative distribution of income. A Gini coefficient of 0.0 would correspond to an equal distribution of income among everyone in a country. One of 1.0 would result if all the income in a country were held by one person. Actual distributions range from between 0.25 and 0.3 in Spain and Finland and 0.6 in some countries of Latin America. Reproduced by permission of the Inter-American Development Bank. See Inter-American Development Bank, *Facing Up to Inequality in Latin America*, p. 11.

is.[53] Considering that migration is driven by relative differences in income between sending countries and receiving countries and crime is associated with poverty, then the inequitable distribution of income prevalent in Latin America contributes to both migration and crime by increasing the number of people living at the low end of the income distribution.

From their extensive econometric analysis of the relationship between inequality and violent crime, Pablo Fajnzylber, Daniel Lederman, and Norman Loayza concluded that

> an increase in income inequality has a significant and robust effect of raising crime rates. In addition, the GDP growth rate has a significant crime-reducing impact. Since the rate of growth and distribution of income jointly determine the rate of poverty reduction, the two aforementioned results imply that the rate of poverty alleviation has a crime-reducing effect.[54]

Their results underscore the security relevance of the main focus of this paper, short-term economic performance, as well as the longer-term security consequences of patterns of income distribution.

The difficulty of changing the distribution of income is not trivial, as illustrated by the stubborn resistance in the U.S. economy to several efforts to reduce disparities in distribution, starting with the New Deal in the 1930s and continuing in the programs of the Great Society of the 1960s and since. Efforts in Latin America to use the tax system to redistribute income have frequently done more to demonstrate the weakness of governmental authority and the political power of the privileged than to change incomes. The current attempts of Hugo Chávez to redistribute income through social programs in Venezuela have also illustrated that care must be taken to avoid scaring investors, causing them not to undertake new projects and thereby reducing the income available to almost everyone.

So what remedies are left? They come down to long-term solutions that empower people politically and economically. Broadening the franchise, enhancing the independence and objectivity of the judiciary, and giving citizens better opportunities to increase their incomes would help. An approach that potentially impacts all of these objectives is education, and the Inter-American Development Bank and many governments are redoubling their efforts in this area. Education is not as politically sensitive as land reform or other explicit programs that depend on virtually zero-sum redistribution of wealth or income. In fact, even privileged members of a society can benefit from the improvement to civic culture that accompanies better educational achievement by the neediest citizens.

Latin America as a region has ample room for improvement in education. The average Latin American over twenty-five years of age had 4.8 years of education in the early 1990s, compared with more than six years in the Asian "miracle" countries. Large variations existed among countries in the region. At one extreme, approximately half the population in Guatemala and Haiti had no education, while the average adult had less than three years of schooling. At the other extreme, countries like Chile and Argentina averaged more than eight years, near the level of industrialized countries. Adults in the most populous Latin American countries, Brazil and Mexico, had averages close to five years of school.[55]

The case of Chile provides encouragement that poverty can be reduced. In combining targeted social programs with economic stability and high levels of economic growth, three successive democratic governments were able to reduce the incidence of poverty from 40 percent in 1987 to 17 percent in 1998. Investments in human capital and social protection achieved levels of social indicators such as enrollment in primary education, youth literacy, infant mortality, and life expectancy similar to those common in industrialized countries. Despite these advances, however, Chile remains a country of severe disparities in income distribution and marked differences among demographic groups, with indigenous populations, youth, female-headed households, and rural residents especially vulnerable.[56]

Distributive policies cannot be seen as a substitute for economic measures that produce healthy rates of growth. In fact, redistribution should be easier in conditions of good growth. The best way to improve distribution of income in the short run is to provide employment opportunities for the poorest sectors of an economy. An Argentine economist, Agustín Monteverde, addressed the issue of growth and income distribution in this way:

> The central problem for Argentina, at least, is to recreate the conditions to produce wealth. The country has suffered a long and deep decline in productivity over the last sixty years.
>
> Problems of income distribution are worse in other countries of the region. If, through a framework of stable rules of the game and more open competition, Argentina will be able to recoup investment and savings and, consequently, productivity, it will thus also be able to improve the distribution of income.[57]

Care must be taken, though, lest governments treat temporary improvements in the income of their less advantaged citizens as a reason to avoid the politically tough decisions required to implement other measures to improve income distribution. In the long term, structural change will be required.

The precise effect of poor income distribution on the security issues that we have been discussing may be harder to predict than the effects of short-term declines in macroeconomic performance. People are likely to react at a given moment to a worsening in their perceived economic status, especially if it involves unemployment or inflation, either of which can produce sharp declines in purchasing power. One should not, however, underestimate the potentially negative consequences of a situation that ordinary citizens can perceive as lacking either social justice or the incentive to strive and produce that comes from a strong relationship between effort and reward.

Conclusion and Policy Recommendations

The foregoing assessment leads to a conclusion that poor economic performance often has nearly immediate security consequences, such as the civil disturbances caused by the economic collapse in Argentina. Sometimes the expected consequences may not materialize, as in the matter of support for democracy in the face of economic crises in Venezuela and Argentina. Migration is tied to economic disparities, but the security impact of this phenomenon may not be significant unless illegal immigration provides a conduit for infiltration of terrorists. Crime is correlated with both economic performance and distribution of income.

Surely security problems can flow from factors other than economic performance, such as crime, corruption, or terrorism. Assessment of the contribution of economic factors to security problems can be difficult, and some issues merit further research. Among

TABLE 3

Summary of Policy Recommendations for the United States and Latin America

	UNITED STATES	LATIN AMERICA
Security	Pay attention. There is a security problem, but like the War on Terrorism, the threats are not primarily from other states.	Recognize the interconnectedness among political, economic, and security challenges.
Diplomacy	Adopt a more inclusive posture and rhetoric. With the current, unprecedented consensus on fundamentals, it is safe to consult with Latin Americans.	Avoid the temptation to score debating points against the United States when serious national interests are not at stake. Try to apply democratic standards consistently.
Economic Policy	Maintain a strong rate of economic growth and reduce barriers to imports of goods of interest to Latin America.	While seeking short-term growth, also invest in programs that offer improvement in the distribution of income even if results will come only in the long term.
Trade	Negotiate a Free Trade Area of the Americas that meets the need for progress on access to the U.S. market for Latin American agricultural exports.	Acknowledge the U.S. need for concessions from the European Union before domestic supports for agriculture can be terminated. Seek agreement on agricultural provisions that would be conditioned on progress in the Doha Round. Negotiate a termination of export subsidies in the Western Hemisphere.

these topics are the relationships between short-term economic performance, on the one hand, and migratory flows and security budgets on the other.

One thing is clear: economic downturns do nothing to improve security. The foregoing analysis leads naturally to several recommendations for policy makers both in the United States and in Latin America.

U.S.–Latin American relations and cooperation suffer from a kind of attention deficit disorder, which manifests itself differently north and south of the Rio Grande. On the U.S. side of that border there is a tendency to think about Latin America only when a serious threat to U.S. security emanates from the region. Fidel Castro was correct when he claimed credit for creating the Alliance for Progress. President John F. Kennedy would not have proposed, and Congress would not have approved, the largest assistance program in hemispheric history if there had not been a strong perception that Castro's brand of armed revolution posed a serious danger to stability and to other U.S. interests. Similarly, the second-largest U.S. assistance effort and the creation, under the Caribbean Basin Initiative, of a system to allow goods from Central America and the Caribbean to be imported duty-free into the United States were responses to the threat posed by a Marxist government in Nicaragua and active revolutionary groups in El Salvador and Guatemala during the 1980s. Currently, security and narcotics threats drive a massive U.S. commitment to Plan Colombia.

For Latin Americans, the degree of U.S. attention veers between too much and too little. The history of U.S.–Latin American relations is littered with the residue of military interventions—some welcome, many not, especially after the fact. There is a widespread perception in Latin America that the attention of the United States has been diverted elsewhere by the events of 11 September and the war on terrorism. Currently, when the United States does show concern about Latin America, with the notable exception of Plan Colombia, its interest is seen to be mainly commercial. When this perception colors U.S. attention as selective and one-dimensional, it casts suspicion on the interest of the United States in creating a Free Trade Area of the Americas (FTAA), a fear that Washington is only seeking commercial advantage. In contrast, U.S. supporters of an FTAA are more likely to see the benefits as reciprocal among participating countries and extending beyond commerce to improving political and security conditions.

What means are available to escape this box? For the United States, it would help to give greater recognition to the fact that hemispheric security can be threatened by unsatisfactory economic performance, poor governance, or a skewed distribution of income. This realization could undergird a policy of greater engagement with countries of the hemisphere and perhaps permit problems to be addressed while they are in an early stage and can be more easily managed. This approach is compatible with the War on Terrorism, in which threats come less from other nation states, as in the past, and more from individuals, groups, and networks of adversaries.

For Latin American leaders, more emphasis on the interconnectedness among political, economic, and security challenges might suggest ways for greater cooperation within Latin America and more constructive relations with Washington. The United States could facilitate this dynamic diplomatically by adopting a more inclusive posture and more constructive rhetoric. Despite some continuing irritants, there has not been a broader consensus from Alaska to Tierra del Fuego on the basic tenets of democratic governance and market-oriented economic policy for at least decades and perhaps in the history of the hemisphere. Thus dialogue should be easier than ever and freer of risk. Washington can afford to consult as an equal with other countries in the hemisphere—for example, in formulating responses to threats to democracy such as those seen recently in Venezuela and Bolivia.

Latin American leaders can encourage this process by working to find the common ground that they share with the United States and to articulate common policies. They should resist two temptations. One is the appeal of scoring debating points against a powerful United States on issues outside the Western Hemisphere—say in the Middle East—that may have little salience in the country making the point but are perceived as vital by the United States. A similar temptation is the desire to honor a leader, Fidel

Castro, who has never been a democrat but whose success in standing up to the United States has made him a popular figure in many Latin American quarters. To overlook Castro's record on human rights and his other political shortcomings does more than annoy the United States. It undermines the accomplishments of those who have fought for and achieved democratic progress elsewhere in the hemisphere, and it saps the legitimacy on which further democratic consolidation must be based.

U.S. security objectives, as well as broad objectives of economic and political progress, can be served by measures that strengthen economic performance in the hemisphere. The most important contribution the United States can make to this end is something it wants to do anyway. Maintaining a strong rate of growth in the U.S. economy will do more than anything else to provide opportunities for increased exports and new investment that will improve economic performance in Latin America. Latin American leaders will also wish to do all they can to promote strong economic growth. As they focus naturally on the near term, they should also make investments in education or other programs that will improve the distribution of income. Governments will of course realize that progress on improving income distribution will take time and significant results will not likely be realized during their terms in office. History will reward foresighted leadership, and capable leaders will be able to educate their publics to the fact that their societies will become more secure as less advantaged citizens gain a greater ability to progress economically.

The next thing the United States can do to help is to reduce barriers to the importation of products of special interest to Latin America. This approach was furthered by the elimination late in 2003 of the temporary steel limits imposed in March 2002. Now required is better import treatment for agricultural goods, like sugar and orange juice, which are high Latin American priorities in negotiations on an FTAA. Ultimately, U.S. agricultural supports and export subsidies will have to be rolled back. Even though U.S. negotiators naturally want to win agricultural concessions from the European Union in exchange for reducing U.S. agricultural supports, Latin Americans will continue to see the United States as unsympathetic to their interests unless this change can be accomplished.

Latin American leaders know that the primary objective of the United States in agricultural negotiations in the Doha Round is to achieve a reduction in the high export subsidies and domestic supports employed by the European Union. The United States will not curtail its subsidies and supports absent progress toward eliminating the European programs. It should be possible, though, for Latin American and U.S. negotiators to reach an understanding on U.S. agricultural concessions of interest to Latin America that would be granted when global negotiations made substantive progress on agricultural measures. A benefit of this approach would be to make obvious the common interests of Latin America and the United States in creating a trading environment relatively free of intervention in agricultural markets. If Latin American governments were willing to undertake the ambitious step of countervailing European subsidies or banning agricultural imports from Europe, an agreement to terminate export subsidies on agricultural trade within the Western Hemisphere could be concluded without waiting for completion of the Doha Round of multilateral trade negotiations. The foreign policy benefits would be positive for both Latin America and the United States. The United States would gain goodwill in Latin America, the benefits of regional free trade, and allies against the agricultural policies of the European Union. Latin Americans would get improved access to the huge U.S. market and leverage against the European policies that also retard growth in Latin American exports.

Notes

1. Bernard Brodie, *War and Politics* (New York: Macmillan; London: Collier Macmillan, 1973), p. 344.

2. Paul Kennedy, *The Rise and Fall of the Great Powers* (New York: Vintage House, 1987), p. xvi.

3. For an extensive analysis of the relationship between perceptions and political violence, see Ted Robert Gurr, *Why Men Rebel* (Princeton, N.J.: Princeton Univ. Press for the Center of International Studies of Princeton University, 1970).

4. Agustín Monteverde, personal correspondence, 12 October 2003.

5. "Foreign Direct Investment Flows into Latin America and the Caribbean 2002," *CEPAL News* 23, no. 4 (April 2003).

6. Dani Rodrik, "Why Is There So Much Economic Insecurity in Latin America?" (paper prepared for the World Bank, revised October 1999).

7. OECD, *First Estimate for GDP in the OECD Area, Fourth Quarter of 2002* (Paris: 17 March 2003).

8. Paula J. Dobriansky, Under Secretary of State for Global Affairs, remarks to Association of American Chambers of Commerce in Latin America, 35th Annual Meeting, and 2002 Forecast on Latin America and the Caribbean (Washington, D.C., 8 May 2002).

9. For a debate over the applicability of the Washington Consensus in Latin America, see John Williamson, "What Washington Means by Policy Reform," in *Latin American Adjustment: How Much Has Happened?* ed. John Williamson (Washington, D.C.: Institute for International Economics, 1990); and Moises Naim, "Fads and Fashion in Economic Reforms: Washington Consensus or Washington Confusion?" (remarks at International Conference on Second Generation Reforms, Washington, D.C., 1999).

10. Latinobarómetro, as cited in *The Economist*, 1 November 2003, p. 33.

11. Colin L. Powell, U.S. Secretary of State, intervention at the Plenary of the General Assembly of the Organization of American States (Santiago, Chile, 9 June 2003).

12. Inter-American Dialogue, *The Troubled Americas*, Policy Report 2003 (Sol M. Linowitz Forum), p. 17.

13. "The Stubborn Survival of Frustrated Democrats," *The Economist*, 1 November 2003, p. 33.

14. Andrés Benavente Urbina, "Rupturismo Social y Vulnerabilidad de las Instituciones en America Latina" (paper presented to the Conference on Building Regional Security in the Western Hemisphere, sponsored by the Dante B. Fascell North-South Center of the University of Miami, U.S. Army War College, and U.S. Southern Command, 2–4 March 2003) (author's translation).

15. Richard L. Millett, *Colombia's Conflicts: The Spillover Effects of a Wider War* (Miami, Fla.: Strategic Studies Institute of the U.S. Army War College and Dante B. Fascell North-South Center of the University of Miami, October 2002), p. 30.

16. "Superman Uribe Holds Back the Tide," *The Economist*, 7 June 2003, p. 30.

17. For one example, see Dennis P. Rempe, *The Past as Prologue? A History of U.S. Counterinsurgency Policy in Colombia, 1958–1966* (Miami, Fla.: Strategic Studies Institute of U.S. Army War College and Dante B. Fascell North-South Center of the University of Miami, October 2002), p. 31.

18. Luz E. Nagle, *Plan Colombia: Reality of the Colombian Crisis and Implications for Hemispheric Security* (Miami, Fla.: Strategic Studies Institute of the U.S. Army War College and Dante B. Fascell North-South Center of the University of Miami, October 2002), p. 3.

19. Ibid., p. 34.

20. "A Decline without Parallel," *The Economist*, 2 March 2002, p. 26.

21. Larry Rohter, "Once Secure, Argentines Now Lack for Food and Hope," *New York Times*, 3 March 2002, p. 6.

22. Julio Cirino, 13 November 2002.

23. Luis Bitencourt, *Brazil's Growing Insecurity: Is It a Threat to Brazilian Democracy?* Policy Papers on the Americas, vol. 14, study 1 (Washington, D.C.: Center for Strategic and International Studies, 2003).

24. Ibid., p. 16.

25. Juan Forero, "As Venezuela Slides, the Poor Stand By Their Man," *New York Times*, 30 April 2003, p. A3.

26. For an expert analysis of the Bolivarian Circles and other aspects of the Venezuelan dynamic, see Miguel Diaz, Brian Latell, Kenneth "Buddy" McKay, Jr., José Sorzano, and Alexander

Watson, *An Assessment of the Current Venezuelan Situation and Recommendations for the Future*, Policy Papers on the Americas, vol. 12,
study 6 (Washington, D.C.: Center for Strategic
and International Studies, July 2002).

27. Ibid.

28. Forero, "As Venezuela Slides, the Poor Stand
By Their Man."

29. Quoted in Larry Rohter, "Letter from the
Americas: Grievances That Can Bring Globalization to Grief," *New York Times*, 5 November 2003, p. A4.

30. Ibid.

31. Larry Rohter, "Bolivian Leader's Ouster Seen
as Warning on U.S. Drug Policy," *New York
Times*, 23 November 2003, p. A1.

32. Quoted in Larry Rohter, "Bolivia's Poor Proclaim Abiding Distrust of Globalization," *New
York Times*, 17 October 2003, p. A3.

33. "Arequipa's Anger, Peru's Problem," *The
Economist*, 22 June 2002, p. 33.

34. Inter-American Development Bank, "IDB
Study Warns of Disillusionment with Democracy," 9 March 2002.

35. Johann Graf Lambsdorff, "2002 Corruption
Perceptions Index," in Transparency International, *Global Corruption Report: Covering
Worldwide Corruption from July 2001 to June
2000*, pp. 262–65.

36. Paul Constance, "Secrecy Is a Form of Corruption," *IDB America* (February 2001).

37. "The Longest Journey: A Survey of Migration," *The Economist*, 2 November 2002, p. 6.

38. Economic Commission for Latin America and
the Caribbean [hereafter ECLAC], "Almost
Twenty Million Latinamericans and
Caribbeans Are Migrants," press release, 20
November 2002.

39. U.S. Census Bureau, *The Foreign Born Population in the United States: March 2002*, p. 2.

40. ECLAC, "Almost Twenty Million Latinamericans and Caribbeans Are Migrants," p. 2.

41. Ibid.

42. Monteverde, personal correspondence.

43. Ibid.

44. ECLAC, *Globalization and Development*, LC/
G.2157 (SES.29/3) (presented at Brasilia,
Brazil, 6–10 May 2002), p. 250.

45. "Opening the Door," *The Economist*, 2 November 2002, p. 11.

46. International Organization for Migration,
"Trafficking in Migrants: Some Global and
Regional Perspectives" (paper submitted for
the Regional Conference on Migrations,
Puebla, Mexico, 13–14 March 1996), quoted
by Peter Andreas, "Smuggling Wars: Law En-
forcement and Law Evasion in a Changing
World," in *Transnational Crime in the Americas:
An Inter-American Dialogue Book*, ed. Tom Farer
(New York: Routledge, 1999), p. 96.

47. Andrés Solimano, *Remittances by Emigrants:
Issues and Evidence* (Santiago: Economic
Commission for Latin America and the Carib-
bean, 2003), p. 31.

48. Latinobarómetro, as cited in *The Economist*, 1
November 2003, p. 34.

49. That this approach was not the only option
commended to the president is illustrated by
the debate within the Bush administration
that Constantine C. Menges, a former aide in
the Reagan White House, triggered with his op-
ed piece in the *Washington Times* on 12 September 2002, entitled "Blocking a New Axis of Evil"
(led by Castro, Chávez, and da Silva).

50. Inter-American Development Bank, *Facing
Up to Inequality in Latin America: Economic
and Social Progress in Latin America, 1998–
1999 Report*. The source for these comparisons
is the database in Deininger and Squire (1996),
which has information on income distribution
based on reliable household surveys in 108
countries. Southeast Asia includes only Hong
Kong, Korea, Singapore, and Taiwan.

51. Ibid., p. 22.

52. Ibid., p. 23.

53. Ibid., p. 22.

54. Pablo Fajnzylber, Daniel Lederman, and Norman Loayza, "Inequality and Violent Crime,"
Journal of Law and Economics (April 2002), p. 7.

55. All data in this paragraph are from IDB, *Facing
Up to Inequality in Latin America*, pp. 45–47.

56. The World Bank Group, "Country Brief:
Chile," available at 1nweb18.worldbank.org/
external/lac/lac.nsf/Countries/Chile/
71BC8229DD493B2A8, p. 1.

57. Monteverde, personal correspondence.

CHAPTER THREE

Chinese Interests in Latin America

GUILLERMO R. DELAMER, LYLE J. GOLDSTEIN, JORGE EDUARDO
MALENA, AND GABRIELA E. PORN

China's power is on the rise. The reverberations of this critical twenty-first-century
phenomenon are now starting to be felt in all regions of the world, from the Middle
East to Africa, and even in more distant Latin America. While data on the latter topic
remain sparse and preliminary in nature, this chapter represents a first attempt to analyze China's emerging interests in Latin America.

What once was a heated debate among scholars has yielded to a firm consensus on
China's gradually increasing weight in international affairs. Beijing's recent achieve-
ments are most evident in the sphere of economic development. Predictions of an economic meltdown resulting from a weak banking system have not come to pass. Instead,
Beijing capably navigated the Asian financial crisis of the late 1990s, and also the impact of the 2003 Severe Acute Respiratory Syndrome (SARS) epidemic. Especially in
the wake of its entry into the World Trade Organization (WTO) in late 2001, China's
growth projections for the foreseeable future are robust.

China's new power is not restricted to the economic realm, however. Indeed, Beijing
has emerged as an important voice on issues ranging from the future of Afghanistan, to
the Iraq question, to the immense challenge of denuclearizing the Korean Peninsula.
China's active diplomacy in the latter crisis has led some China watchers to herald a
new era of responsible and cooperative Chinese diplomacy. The interpretation has
been given additional impetus by what has been widely described as a major "charm
offensive," directed chiefly at important proximate states such as South Korea and Aus-
tralia. These hopeful appraisals, however, are challenged to some extent by the realization that a not insignificant proportion of China's new wealth is fueling an ambitious
program of military modernization.

If Beijing's ambitions grow in tandem with its capabilities (as has been the case with all
other great powers), the geopolitical ramifications of China's emergence could be felt
in every corner of the globe. Moreover, China has been adopting omnidirectional

initiatives toward all regions throughout the world. No doubt its primary objective has been the search for new markets, but Beijing is also seeking the promotion of greater international multipolarization. Consistent with the foregoing analysis, specialists have begun to consider China's growing activities in regions outside the confines of East Asia. China's emerging roles in South Asia, Central Asia, the Middle East, Africa, and Europe are now receiving regular and careful scrutiny. A noteworthy exception is China's developing relations with Latin America. The purpose of this chapter is to assess the nature and extent of Chinese activity in Latin America and its strategic implications for hemispheric security.

The chapter concludes that at this time, Chinese activity in Latin America is largely confined to seeking out expanded trade opportunities. While the PRC also supports a general policy of multipolarization, there is no evidence of an emerging Chinese threat to this region. Washington and other regional states will still want to monitor certain sensitive issues closely, for example, Sino-Cuban relations and Chinese commercial acquisitions in the Panama Canal region; but the overall picture is one of benign expansion, characterized by increasing trade and cooperation with the states of Latin America.

The analysis begins with a broad examination of China's foreign-policy decision-making structure; this is followed by a discussion of the new leadership's evolution and general policy directions. This background forms an essential context for the subsequent description of Chinese interests in Latin America; readers familiar with Chinese foreign-policy practices may want to skip ahead to that section. A final section explores China's relations with Argentina in some detail, as a "case study" for Beijing's emerging diplomacy in Latin America.

PRC Foreign-Policy Decision Making

China is a socialist state, where actual power differs from formal power. The Chinese Communist Party (CCP) leads and directs all actual governing processes. The Standing Committee of the politburo represents the core of true power in Beijing, and its members are the leaders who set the overall direction of the party, government, and armed forces. Within the Standing Committee is the Foreign Affairs Leadership Group (FALG), which is in charge of assessing and making decisions on international issues. This working group is supported by four key ministries, including Foreign Affairs (Li Zhaoxing), Foreign Trade and Economic Cooperation (Lu Fuyuan), Defense (Cao Guangchuan), and Intelligence (Xu Yongyue). If a matter involving Latin America arises, it falls under the responsibilities of one of seven divisions, denominated "America and Oceania," supported by a Directorate for Latin American Affairs.

The People's Liberation Army (PLA) is also part of the FALG, through its chief of staff, General Liang Guanglie. It is noteworthy that China's Ministry of Defense has an "American/Oceania Bureau," but the General Staff has no special bureau designated to cover Latin America, whereas it does have bureaus for other regions of particular concern, including North America, Europe, West Asia, and Africa.[1]

When dealing with specific decision-making issues related to Chinese–Latin American matters, the FALG calls upon two agencies. From the national government apparatus, there is the Foreign Affairs Ministry Directorate for Latin America, to which the General Directorate for America and Oceania (led by He Yafei) is subordinated. From the academic subsystem's side, there is the Institute for Latin American Studies (led by Li Mingde), which is part of the Chinese Social Sciences Academy.

Possible Evolution of the Chinese Power Structure

China undertook an important shift of leading figures within its internal power structure during 2002–2003. China's new leadership, including, most prominently, President Hu Jintao and Prime Minister Wen Jiabao, is described as China's "Fourth Generation" leadership. The new leaders have common characteristics, such as coming of age during Mao's catastrophic Cultural Revolution. They are, as a result, more pragmatic and much less ideologically imbued than their predecessors, but they also retain strong nationalist convictions.

The Fourth Generation is mainly made up of technocrats who have climbed the central and local bureaucratic ladders by making use of their specialized knowledge. The Third Generation leaders specialized in the "hard sciences"—most of them were engineers—but the Fourth Generation is characterized by an abundance of economists and lawyers. This trend shows that new leaders are leaning toward the social sciences, which might indicate profound changes on China's political horizon. The Fourth Generation leadership is noteworthy in that it completely lacks military experience.

There is no doubting that the new leaders are a generation of political reformers. They will most likely fight widespread corruption and nepotism by opening up the Party's membership to private entrepreneurs and business executives. This does not necessarily imply that they will become "pro-Western," however, because they appear to have strong nationalist tendencies. They visualize the Party as a means to an end, facilitating control over China's vast population and maintaining conditions of stability and growth.

On the one hand, Beijing has sought to cooperate with Washington in the new War on Terror. For instance, China fully supported Operation ENDURING FREEDOM and also has engaged in counterterrorism cooperation with the United States. On the other hand, China recently has felt itself encircled by U.S. military forces, now deployed in nearby areas such as Kyrgyzstan and the Philippines. Therefore, Beijing may well seek to compensate for Washington's geopolitical gains by accelerating economic development and elevating national security as a national priority.

To mitigate the tremendous influence exercised by the only superpower remaining after the end of the Cold War—namely, the United States—the new generation of leaders in China will very likely try to enhance their relations not only with their immediate neighbors but also with Europe, the Middle East, Africa, and Latin America. To date, China's vital objectives continue to emphasize economic development objectives: the improvement of rural living standards and energy-sector infrastructure, and the development of high technology. Beijing knows that achieving these objectives will inevitably require external support and assistance, wherever it can be found.

In sum, China's emergence presents a great unknown for the twenty-first century and beyond. While its strategic orientation has tended to be defensive and rather narrowly focused on guarding its own sovereignty, it is difficult to predict whether a more capable China will adhere to this paradigm. On the other hand, it is quite certain that China's internal development will experience instability and difficulties in the further development of a modern state and economy. Domestic uncertainties may in turn precipitate unsettling changes in Chinese foreign and security policies.

China's Strategy and Policy over the Coming Years

In the political arena, China professes a desire to act responsibly as a great nation, playing an important role in safeguarding peace and international security by promoting justice and equality. Beijing opposes hegemonic practices or the use of force by powerful nations to impose their will on the rest of the international community.

China promulgates the so-called Five Principles of Peaceful Coexistence for creating a "new" international order: one more balanced, peaceful, and fair; one where mutual respect for sovereignty and territorial integrity is maintained; one without aggression, without interference in domestic affairs, and with peaceful coexistence as well as equality for all, to achieve mutual benefits through cooperation and common development.

During the 1990s, many in Beijing perceived that Washington often acted arrogantly toward the PRC, injuring China's national pride, violating its sovereignty, and seeking to weaken its international influence among other nations. They also viewed the United States as arrogant, "obsessed" with freedom and democracy, guided by a mission to change the communist regime that governs the country, and desirous of playing the role of "world policeman."[2]

Many Chinese admit that they do not live in a democratic society according to Western standards, but at the same time they recognize that, considering the immense size of their country, its geography, and its difficult historical circumstances, China has made great strides, especially in the last two decades. The PRC economy has undergone important changes, growing at an average of 7 to 8 percent a year, and "corrupting" the cornerstones of the communist ideology and structure by, among other things, developing a new legal system, increasing the power of legislative bodies, forcing government leaders to retire at a certain age, and allowing businesspeople to take part in the Party's structure.

Nevertheless, China's progress regarding human rights has been disappointing, especially given the severe crackdown on the Falun Gong movement. Beyond this group are still many more Chinese who criticize government inefficiency and state bureaucracy but believe that Chinese themselves are capable of solving these problems without any external "advice."

In general, China's current leaders are staunch advocates of social stability. They do not believe in excessively "accelerating" the democratizing process for fear of political and social chaos. They know very well from their history that anarchy has cost China millions of deaths and grave national humiliation. They have also observed how a swift transition from an authoritarian to a democratic system (as in the case of the Soviet Union) can result in social collapse and chaos.

This seems to explain why Chinese now accept restrictions on their freedom and individual rights. A comparison with the much more democratic India, which continues to be fettered by population pressures and unrelieved squalor, yields the tentative conclusion that the Chinese argument may have some merit.

Chinese believe that a multipolar world will emerge at some point, but they do not deny that the world is currently unipolar, with only one dominating superpower. Some Chinese feel that the United States has taken advantage of the historical "opportunity" presented by the War on Terror to adopt an offensive, neoimperialistic, and interventionist national strategy that allows it to secure world supremacy. They sense that the United States uses international organizations to weaken and isolate certain countries, manipulating international laws, rules, and standards, and adopting the traditional "gunboat diplomacy" approach, in search of a new "containment" strategy toward nations such as China, which is undergoing successful development and could, therefore, become a peer competitor in the future.

Chinese grand strategy currently focuses on striking a balance between two often opposing objectives. The first is developing "comprehensive national power," which includes a qualitative and quantitative assessment of political, economic, military, scientific, technological, and foreign affairs issues so as to determine relative power among nations. The other objective is the maximum exploitation of what Chinese call *shi,* or the "strategic configuration of power," based on Sun Tzu's millenarian theories.[3] Chinese explain it by saying that it refers to the alignment of forces or the "(natural) tendency of things" and say that a skillful strategist can exploit it to attain victory. This concept, so it is maintained, will allow them to preserve their national independence and contribute to China's momentum in its effort to increase its national power.[4]

China's grand strategy revolves around the following pillars:

- Contribute to the creation of a peaceful international environment so that China can focus on its economic development.
- Attain Taiwan's national reunification.
- Increase the scope (magnitude) of national power to build a Chinese pole within a desired multipolar world future.
- Build a new international political and economic order with less power and wealth inequality between rich and poor and more relevance to the principle of sovereignty.[5]

China has adopted omnidirectional initiatives toward all regions of the world. Its primary objective has been the search for new markets, seeking new options and the promotion of greater international multipolarization. Beijing has been patiently but unrelentingly establishing tighter ties with third-world countries by encouraging greater pluralism in terms of power.[6]

China is aware that the United States could label it as an "adversary" and is making efforts not to be placed in that category by avoiding any confrontation. This policy corresponds to China's highest security interests, depicted in a long-term strategy.[7] The country's leaders seem to have concluded that it would make no sense to confront the United States (at least in the near term) since it would lead them to international isolation, a situation Beijing is anxious to avoid. On the other hand, some scholars interpret the recent warming in U.S.-China relations as a conscious effort by the Chinese leadership to husband its strength during a "strategic pause," while the United States is distracted by conflict in the Middle East and elsewhere. Unfortunately, a sudden reversal in Chinese policy that would seek to take advantage of America's distractions, while perhaps unlikely, cannot be ruled out.

Economic Policies

China realizes that significant changes are taking place in the world economy and accordingly has become more global and more economically competitive, so as to gain new markets, financing, and resources. In addition, Chinese transnational companies have gained increased market share. Beijing is also aware that globalization has transformed what in the past was an era of trade among nations into a new era where transnational production prevails. Beijing has accepted the fact that scientific and technological progress and innovation are changing production modalities, in which knowledge has become the true driving force behind economic growth.

As a consequence of economic liberalization, which has permitted China to sustain high growth rates, new phenomena have appeared, such as unemployment and subemployment. There are over one hundred million unemployed people, a fact that could unleash significant social pressures. Large and volatile protests by angry workers, especially in China's "rust belt" in the northeast, are becoming more and more common.[8] A related development is the evolution of a very large class of poor internal migrants who have moved illegally into China's large cities in search of work. This same problem has also generated a huge increase in illegal activities, especially drug trafficking, gambling, prostitution, pickpocketing, and other crimes.

Defense Policies

China is implementing a campaign to generate profound changes in its defense system, in terms of both its capabilities and its image. Aware that its military equipment is technologically inferior to that of developed countries, in particular the United States, the PLA has been downsizing its active duty personnel and has been seeking to develop specialized troops and new tactics.

To avoid creating suspicion among neighboring countries and other countries around the world, the PLA has simultaneously carried out a full doctrine review to increase transparency regarding its plans and military equipment. One of the methods employed to this end has been increased military-to-military contacts with Asian nations and the rest of the world as well.

Thus, Chinese military delegations have been making regular visits to Argentina, interested in gaining expertise in various areas ranging from the handling of equipment and ordnance to personnel management, selection, and evaluation processes. The PLA has recently opened up its military bases to journalists and shown their facilities and their way of life to the public. It is also proud to say that China has no imperialist intentions whatsoever and that, given the country's position of technological inferiority, it does not pose a risk to other countries. Despite measured progress in enhancing transparency, many significant questions regarding the PLA remain shrouded in mystery and speculation; not the least of these is the problem of China's actual defense expenditures. Indeed, the true figure is estimated to be many times greater than the modest official figure.

China's continuing naval development facilitates its new military diplomacy. For the first time in its naval history, a small People's Liberation Army Navy (PLAN) flotilla circumnavigated the world in 2002. The missile destroyer *Qingdao* was accompanied on the tour by the logistics vessel *Taicang*. The ships visited Singapore, Egypt, Turkey, Ukraine, Greece, Portugal, Brazil, Ecuador, and Peru. Clearly, Beijing believes that it is now more useful to remain open, instead of isolating itself from the outside world and raising suspicions regarding its intentions. Certainly, Chinese leaders want to change their image, internally and externally, to leave behind the "Tiananmen Square Syndrome."

Despite these positive developments, caution is warranted, because China's military modernization appears to be progressing rapidly. As part of a new aerospace-maritime orientation—the strategic consequence of China's largely pacified land borders—Beijing is making significant investments, especially in Russian armaments. New purchases include a second batch of *Sovremenny*-class destroyers, eight new *Kilo*-class submarines, fighter-bombers specifically configured for maritime operations, and radar aircraft to provide over-the-horizon targeting. These programs are complemented by co-production agreements, in addition to indigenous production programs, that parallel almost all large purchases. Russian scientists admit that they may eventually be outclassed by Chinese defense science, which is rapidly improving. China's large and increasingly sophisticated short-range missile force is evidence of this development. Beijing is also undertaking a major effort to modernize its nuclear forces. At the same time, training is undergoing a genuine revolution as the PLA integrates competitive "red versus blue" exercises that encourage commanders to make "on the spot" judgments. Along with reforms in recruiting and military education, such measures have the potential to make the PLA a formidable future opponent, especially in the East Asian littoral.

Chinese Foreign Policy and Latin America

The PRC views Latin America as a marginal or peripheral region in political and economic terms. The absence of a settled and stable security structure in East Asia, in addition to its still-limited capacities, obliges China to focus its diplomatic efforts mainly on its neighbors for the time being.

As a result of this focus, Beijing has generally left aside regions that are geographically distant from China or have little international influence. Among the states of the developing world, China has pursued ties in Africa rather aggressively. Beijing's long-standing criticism of imperialism, together with its refusal to consider the human rights situation in partner countries, has enabled it to establish strong bilateral ties with such strategically significant states as Nigeria, South Africa, Sudan, and Egypt.[9] By contrast, Latin America appears to be a lower priority, perhaps owing to the region's strong identification with the West. However, the fact that several Latin American countries continue to confer diplomatic status to Taiwan as an independent nation was and still is a matter of concern to Beijing.

The Latin American and Caribbean countries that maintain diplomatic relations with the PRC (and dates on which they became official) are: Cuba (28 September 1960); Chile (15 December 1970); Peru (2 November 1971); Mexico (14 February 1972); Argentina (19 February 1972); Guyana (17 June 1972); Jamaica (21 November 1972); Trinidad and Tobago (20 June 1974); Venezuela (28 June 1974); Brazil (15 August 1974); Suriname (28 May 1972); Barbados (30 May 1977); Ecuador (2 January 1980); Colombia (7 February 1980); Antigua and Barbuda (1 January 1983); Bolivia (9 July 1985); Nicaragua (7 December 1985); Uruguay (3 February 1988); Bahamas (23 May 1997); and Santa Lucia (1 September 1997).

The fourteen Latin American countries that recognize the Republic of China (Taiwan) include Belize, Costa Rica, Dominica, Dominican Republic, El Salvador, Granada, Guatemala, Haiti, Honduras, Nicaragua, Panama, Paraguay, Saint Kitts and Nevis, and Saint Vincent and the Grenadines. It is important to note that the total number of countries that still recognize Taiwan as an independent nation is only twenty-six, thus underscoring the significance of the proportion of such countries from the Latin American region.

Another issue that has awakened Chinese interest in the region has been the significant weight that Latin America represents as a regional voting block at the UN. This is important to Beijing, for example, in the case of limiting the scrutiny of the UN Human Rights Commission (UNHRC).

The PRC is a permanent member of the United Nations Security Council and in that setting has depicted itself as the representative of third-world countries. However, when the time came to show loyalty toward these countries, it became evident that China consistently privileged its own national interests, as expected, and in so doing, hampered its relations with developing states.

Occasionally, the Chinese press still employs Latin American problems as a propaganda tool against American "hegemonism." For example, a detailed spread in the January 2002 issue of *Guoji Zhanwang* (Shanghai Institute for International Relations) sharply criticizes the U.S. training program for Latin American military officers under the headline "School for Autocrats."[10] In another relatively recent detailed Chinese survey of Latin America, the authors make no secret of their contention that China and Latin America together face a common struggle against U.S. "hegemonism," nor do they seek to bury the issue of historical PRC support for Latin American revolutionary movements.[11] Of course, these ideological efforts do not compare in size, scope, or ideological distortion with propaganda initiatives undertaken in the Maoist era.

Overshadowing these political factors and any ideological issues, however, is the emergence of the trade factor in Latin American–Chinese relations. Latin America is increasingly vital to China's acquisition of commodities such as copper and other minerals, steel, grains, oil, wool, frozen fish, fish meal, sugar, leather, and chemical substances. China's sales to the region include light industry products, textiles, machinery, toys, and tools.

However, this relationship is not limited to buying and selling products. It also includes the creation of new markets and the introduction of China's companies into South America. As an example, in 2001, Chinese exports to this region reached almost seven billion dollars, and although they represent only 3 percent of its global sales, Beijing enjoys a favorable trade balance of three billion dollars.

Sino-Brazilian trade relations are at the forefront of these trends. When Brazilian president Luiz Inácio Lula da Silva traveled to Beijing in May 2004, he was accompanied by four hundred Brazilian corporate executives. This is understandable given that Sino-Brazilian trade increased an impressive 69 percent in 2003 to $6.7 billion—and was up another 40 percent in the first quarter of 2004. As China announced three billion dollars in new investments for Brazil, the Brazilian government has hinted at up to five billion dollars in expected Brazilian direct foreign investment in China.[12]

At the center of the soaring Sino-Brazilian trade is Beijing's seemingly insatiable appetite for steel. In 2003 China imported 2.4 million tons of Brazilian steel, worth $730 million, making China one of Brazil's top three export destinations. Among other international investors, Baosteel Shanghai will be pumping capital into the Brazilian steel industry with the goal of increasing production capacity by 30 percent over four years. Of course, such close trade links with China entail inevitable risks. For example, upon news in the spring of 2004 that Chinese leaders were seeking to curb lending to slow growth and prevent "overheating," stock prices for Brazilian steel companies sank on the São Paolo Stock Exchange. On the whole, however, investors remain bullish with respect to Sino-Brazilian trade, and Brazilian steel prospects in particular, probably because of Brazil's enormous iron ore reserves.[13] Not coincidentally, Argentine president Néstor Kirchner visited China just a month after Lula—also accompanied by a huge delegation of business executives.

Oil also plays a role in China's commercial strategy for Latin America. In 1993, China became a net oil importer. Already, China's booming consumption of oil appears to have significantly influenced the world price during 2003–2004. PRC demand for oil, moreover, is projected to double by 2015. Over the last decade, the China National Petroleum Corporation has pursued an aggressive purchasing strategy, securing holdings in both Venezuela and Peru, in addition to making major investments in fields from

Central Asia to Africa.[14] The simultaneous souring of U.S. relations with Venezuela during the troubled tenure of President Hugo Chávez, while Beijing's relations with Caracas have blossomed, has raised concerns in some quarters.[15] As yet, however, such anxieties do not rise to the level of national security concerns.

Beijing's economic interests in Latin America are also based on a "South-South" cooperation scheme in the areas of science and technology. Beijing is looking for the most developed countries in the region from which to gain training expertise in various matters and to incorporate into its own research base. This explains its intention to establish relationships with Brazil and Argentina, especially in the aerospace, satellite, nuclear, steel, food processing, and agricultural industries, software development, and telecommunications. Within the sphere of technology transfer, the China-Brazil Earth Resources Satellite (CBERS) project is a special concern, because China is making very significant strides in remote sensing. These efforts may significantly assist the PLA in over-the-horizon targeting, which remains a major obstacle to PLA operations at present.

Paradoxically, the protectionist policies of developed countries and the creation of integration arrangements in their respective areas of economic influence—such as the North American Free Trade Agreement (NAFTA) involving the United States, Canada, Mexico, and the European Union—is the central reason why economic ties between China and Latin America have increased their pace. Notwithstanding the above, China is not expected to make significant investments (beyond Brazilian steel) in this region, at least not until it reaches a level of industrialization that can satisfy its own needs and make it globally competitive—an objective that will take some years to achieve.

In terms of trade, it is worth noting that despite the reasonable increase in trade over the last few decades, there are still some issues that hinder its overall development. In the first place, both China and Latin America benefit from an abundance of raw materials, a fact that does not contribute to trading these items due to an absence of reciprocal markets. Its manufactured goods are also quite similar and do not contribute in this sense either.

Second, both China and Latin America lack capital and significant state-of-the-art technologies. Third, geographical distances impose an important limitation, although some transportation agreements have been signed. The irregularities of maritime routes and the absence of scheduled flights between the two regions have had an adverse impact.

Fourth, both China and Latin America have weak currencies. In China's case, it is the result of the increased demands of its growing economy, and in South America's case, the crisis was generated by its large foreign debt, discouraging it from increasing its bilateral trade beyond advisable thresholds. Fifth, a persistent lack of mutual under-standing limits the interaction; difficulties range from ignorance about cultural and so-cial realities to ignorance regarding opportunities their respective markets could offer, and their respective rules and regulations. Finally, despite the huge efforts China has made in the last two decades, the differences between the economic systems present an additional obstacle to the normal evolution of trade relations.

Therefore, although political and economic contacts have successfully developed within institutional frameworks, they have not yet grown to an extensive scale. The ma-jor visits by both Brazilian and Argentine presidents in 2004, however, could herald a new era in Sino–Latin American trade.

The turnaround made by Chinese diplomacy since the 1980s and its foreign economic policy has generated a Copernican shift in Beijing's relations with the rest of the world. China has become much more predictable, facilitating cooperation despite the fact that Latin American and Chinese economic and political systems are extremely different.

A Chinese specialist on Latin American affairs, Xu Shicheng, recently observed during a presentation in Argentina that for China, Latin America constitutes a promising re-gion in terms of investments.[16] To modernize its economy, China will need a large amount of natural resources, and Latin America has most of them, including oil, iron, copper, wood, and cotton. China has begun to establish textile centers in Latin America. It has also made progress in certain concepts as it has realized that some technologies of high and medium-size categories can be competitive in the Latin American market.

Xu further described the policies proposed by China in its relationship with the region as follows: "reciprocal benefits, the exchange of products to meet mutual needs, learn-ing from each other, compensating for deficiencies and promoting joint development." He explained that the goal is to combine trade with industry, and trade with invest-ments. Xu also mentioned that his country wishes to strengthen international financial ties and cooperation with Latin America so that companies from both sides can have the resources and credit to increase trade. He concluded his presentation by stating that for China, the dispute between developed and Asian countries for the Latin American market will deepen. He referred to the fact that China is aware of some of its problems in tapping the Latin American market, including the low quality of some export prod-ucts and the relatively poor state of service and support functions, as well as a paucity of computer data on this market.

There is no doubt that the introduction of China into the WTO will have a strong im-pact. China will have to open up its markets to a wide variety of products from Latin America. On the other hand, it will no longer be able openly to subsidize certain export goods that unfairly compete in the international market with Latin American products, such as steel. On the domestic front, however, due to China's very low wages and labor costs, the states of Latin America will have to be prepared to compete in areas that are labor-intensive. Overall, if the positive and negative aspects of this relationship are weighed, it is apparent that there is a great benefit from trade increases for both sides.

Security Issues of Concern

Political and ideological problems have receded on the Sino–Latin America agenda, yielding to the primary issue of trade. Nevertheless, there remains a set of unconventional and conventional security questions that merit continuing analytical attention.

The "Triads"

The so-called triads, criminal organizations that currently have achieved a modest level of activity in Latin America, trace their origins back several centuries. Historically, they were actually formed to expel invaders from their territories; subsequently, they came to hold key positions in the power structure of Chinese civilization. In modern times, however, they are associated with criminal, even mafia-like, activities. There have been numerous triads, including "14K," the "Green Gang," the "Red Gang," and Chiu Chau, to name a few, most of which moved to Hong Kong and Taiwan after 1949.

The triads recently gained notoriety as they expanded to cover a wide range of transnational criminal activities such as blackmail, clandestine gambling, heroin trafficking, illegal immigration, and money laundering. It is difficult to gain a deep knowledge of the characteristics and modi operandi of these groups, but a general idea can be ascertained from interviews, in which sources have requested anonymity for fear of retribution. Triads are exceedingly difficult to infiltrate, since they are based on tight ethnic and geographic filial bonds. They are highly sensitive, intuitive organizations that provide a quick counter to any attempt at penetration.

These organizations recruit young people greedy for money, power, and prestige. They have now spread all over the world and have adapted their business to modern times, to include the forging of luxury watches, software, and documents; slavery; and traffic in opium and heroin. These dealings allow them to collect multimillion-dollar sums to fund their activities throughout the world.

One of the most powerful triads in Latin America, the so-called Fu Chin, is named after a town in the province of Fujian, in southern China. Its main business has been trafficking in human beings, and its modus operandi is as follows:

- It provides immigrants with forged documents.

- It directs immigrants to a certain country of destination, which is selected on the basis of mafia business locations.

- It crowds immigrants arriving at their destinations into cellars and forces them to perform clandestine work, often in the clothing industry or the restaurant business.

- The mafia associates with families that have managed to immigrate with some money, which helps it expand its business. These families are often required to pay the mafia a monthly fee in exchange for "protection."

- To exert a tighter control over illegal immigrants, the mafia organizes them according to their origin or dialect and forbids them to mix among themselves.

- It subjects those who refuse to pay the requested fee to a triad code providing for no "second chances." Denunciation is also grounds for death.

- In Argentina alone, where the ethnic Chinese population amounts to just thirty thousand residents, estimates show that only one out of one hundred ethnic Chinese traders dares to denounce acts of intimidation.

- Once a given family has been able to collect more funds, they might obtain the necessary documents to enter the United States, which is often their final destination.

It is worth noting that there is no evidence linking these activities with the PRC government. In fact, whenever illegal immigration incidents have been reported, as in Venezuela in May 2003, Chinese authorities have strongly denied any connection with them.

The activities conducted by criminal organizations of Asian origin have already attained proportions of an "international threat" on account of the organizations' ability and capacity to establish connections all over the world. In fact, they have managed to enter into temporary partnerships with ethnic secret organizations in the Western Hemisphere and, at the same time, have undertaken illegal business activities.

Illegal Immigration

The issue of illegal immigration from China began to attract public attention as a result of certain incidents—for example, when the ship *Golden Venture,* loaded with 286 Chinese immigrants, ran aground off New York on 6 June 1993. The most recent tragic event involved 58 immigrants who were found dead in a lorry container at Dover, England, in June 2000.

There is widespread concern in different countries about the prospects of a massive emigration from China, the most densely populated country in the world. Some countries fear that if such a development were to occur, its impact might destabilize their societies at a time when few economies in the Americas are performing really well.

The practice of human trafficking has now reached a status comparable to that of slavery in the past, and has inevitably become closely associated with international organized crime. Ethnic Chinese involvement in human trafficking appears to be characterized, in particular, by its versatility and flexibility to operate and mutate, with worldwide networks handling the different approaches to a given host country. Immigrants enter the Americas through a combination of maritime, air, and land means, with intermediate stopovers in Canada, Mexico, or countries in Central America or the Caribbean.[17] Willard H. Myers, an expert in Asian organized crime, ascribes much of the illegal immigration in North and South America to Taiwanese triads. These have used Belize, the Dominican Republic, and the Caribbean islands, including Jamaica and Puerto Rico, as bases of operations from which Chinese immigrants can enter the United States.[18]

Chinese immigration is not bad in itself, of course, since it links peoples and cultures closer together, including legal trading activities. The problem lies in the possibility that undesirable elements belonging to supranational criminal organizations may filter in. This apparent risk should not cast a shadow over the above-mentioned advantages of beneficial, controlled immigration that offers economic benefits without precipitating social conflict and instability or jeopardizing state security.

Migratory flows are transnational issues that require much greater scrutiny, especially in the wake of the terrorist attacks of 11 September 2001. However, these issues are difficult to assess, given problems in evaluating the quality of available data. In fact, information sources are not always thoroughly reliable; even more important, incentives and motivations vary from one migratory group to another, and it is very difficult to identify a group's interests accurately.

Today, the Chinese population residing overseas amounts to approximately forty million people. They are a natural link for promoting the expansion of all kinds of trading exchanges between their countries of residence and the "motherland."

Presence in the Tri-Border Area

In the northeast region of Argentina, on the borders of Brazil, Paraguay, and Argentina, there is a tri-border area, also known as the Triple Frontier, where the Chinese community carries out a great deal of activities. Some fifteen thousand Chinese residents live in the Paraguayan city of Ciudad del Este alone.

As an indication of the commercial dynamism of that social segment, the Taiwanese bank Chinatrust established one of its nine international branches in that city, and the first and only one in Latin America (the rest are located in Hong Kong, India, Indonesia, Great Britain, the Philippines, Thailand, Vietnam, and Japan). Back in 1998,

Chinatrust became one of the five foreign banks in Paraguay, together with ING, Lloyd's, ABN Amro, and Citibank.[19]

This dynamism, coupled with the illegal trade of Asian goods, led to the presumed presence of Chinese mafias in the area, which apparently blend in perfectly with villagers. These mafias are believed to have come from mainland China and Taiwan, and their main business is to charge for "protection" services to local Chinese merchants, as well as to collect "taxes" for containers these merchants import from Asia. When the mafias handle the containers themselves, merchants are obliged to buy those goods to avoid retaliation.[20]

An episode that supports the above allegations occurred in June 2001, when a Chinese citizen, Wu Wenhuan, accused of being one of the mafia leaders in the area, was captured in Ciudad del Este. The case appears to have proved that this group used stamps stuck to illegally imported goods to identify the mafia leader who ruled their sale, and his company (Floresta S. A.) was found to have dodged taxes in over six hundred import transactions.[21]

It has also been proven that these mafia groups travel between Ciudad del Este and Foz do Iguaçu and have North American and European passports.[22] The Chinese mafias operating in the region allegedly carried out illegal operations with a terrorist group called Gamaa Islamiya. According to a newspaper investigation article by Brazilian journalist Roberto Godoy, there seem to be at least two organizations involved: the Sung-I and Ming "families."[23]

The Sung-I family, based in the Paraguayan city of Hernandarias, appears to be using three film-developing and electronics shops in Ciudad del Este as a cover. In December 2000, the Sung-I family allegedly sold an ammunition batch to the Gamaa group via a medical equipment shipment en route to Egypt. The Cameroon flagship was intercepted at the Cyprus port of Limassol. The Ming family apparently manages Gamaa funds from Ciudad del Este, through a financial circuit that could include Guyana and the Cayman Islands. Transnational criminal networks rooted in Chinese ethnicity are among many threats of this type confronting the states of Latin America.

Sino-Cuban Relations

China's rapidly improving ties with Cuba are also of some concern. During the Cold War, these ties were strictly limited by the Sino-Soviet conflict. Since the Cold War, however, the relationship has strengthened considerably. The most important Chinese leaders have all visited Cuba, including Jiang Zemin (1993, 2001), Gen Fu Quanyu (2000), Li Peng (1995), and Hu Jintao (1997). Beijing has extended four hundred million dollars in loans to Havana, but is yet to become one of Cuba's major creditors and still ranks rather low on its list of trading partners. There have been rumors that China might take over the Russian signals intelligence center at Lourdes, since Moscow decided to abandon the facility during the fall of 2001. However, there are no credible sources to confirm these rumors, which may have emerged from Russian sources with ulterior motives.[24] A more credible accusation concerns new Chinese arms sales to Cuba. This accusation was leveled by Assistant Secretary of State for East Asian and Pacific Affairs James Kelly during testimony before Congress in mid-2001. Beijing insists that its military supplies to Cuba are of a nonlethal nature, for example, uniforms.[25] While it is difficult to ascertain the true nature of these transfers, it is apparent that any attempt by Beijing to play a "Cuban card" within the larger context of the Taiwan problem (i.e., parallel arms sales, etc.) appears outlandish, at least for the near and medium term. On the other hand, this expanding relationship certainly bears close watching.

PRC Shipping Initiative: Taking Control of the Canal Zone?

Recent developments strongly suggest that China is seeking to develop a shipping strategy to support its foreign-trade activities through resources generated by the shipping industry. In 1996, the government of Panama granted the Panama Port Company (PPC) a contract to operate both access ports to the Panama Canal: Cristóbal on the Caribbean side and Balboa on the Pacific Ocean. The PPC, a subsidiary of the Hong Kong–based company Hutchison Whampoa Limited, is a port operator currently updating the technology at both ports. This company handles 70 percent of the container traffic all over the world. It has now been given the chance to develop what used to be the U.S. naval base at Rodman Point, close to Balboa.

Some American analysts, arguing that this company is linked to the Chinese military, have objected to this agreement. Indeed, it is quite plausible that, although all Chinese companies serve Chinese economic interests, some could currently be used as "screens" or "cover" to hide certain military activities or even others with a dual purpose.

The Hutchison Whampoa company has denied these allegations. The truth of the matter is that, with this investment, China secures some limited control over maritime traffic in the area as well as some degree of influence over how to operate the canal. Of particular concern would be Chinese efforts to sabotage the canal through special operations during war (unfortunately, a rather simple operation); and of somewhat less concern is the value of observing U.S. Navy (USN) activities in general. On the other hand, it should be noted that aircraft carriers are too large to transit the Panama Canal, raising a question as to whether closure of the canal would actually impact a U.S.-China maritime conflict scenario. USN submarine operations, however, which could play an important role in any maritime conflict with China, could be impacted in the most dire scenarios. The effect on Atlantic versus Pacific basing for such critical assets deserves further detailed study and is ongoing.[26] At the same time, it should be noted that the United States would have multiple options for retaliation if Beijing were to attempt to hold the canal hostage.

In the fall of 2002, the Clinton administration assessed the issue and concluded that Chinese ownership of various port facilities in the canal region did not represent a national security threat. Indeed, from an economic standpoint, it is quite feasible that the most important objective could be the use of this company as a means to channel investments and gain control of shipping. Nevertheless, it will be prudent to monitor these developments closely.

Case Study: Argentina's Relations with China

Although links between Argentina and China date back to over four centuries ago, more fluid exchanges were initiated in the nineteenth century over trade and immigration matters. However, from a political standpoint, relations with China gained significant momentum only during the 1980s, as a result of a need to diversify international economic relations and also as a response to the globalization phenomenon.

The Political Dimension of Argentina-China Relations

After the launching of China's reform policy in 1978, Beijing decided to focus strongly on economic growth. As a consequence, the material aspect of the interaction between China and Latin America developed seamlessly, leading to a deepening of political ties and signaling the beginning of the end of China's chronic trade deficit with the region.[27]

Once Argentina returned to democratic governance in 1983, bilateral ties were placed on a firm foundation of friendship and cooperation. Heralding a new era of goodwill, Foreign Minister Wu Xueqian visited Buenos Aires in April 1984 and signed a cultural exchange agreement. A year later, Dante Caputo, the Argentine foreign minister, traveled to Beijing and signed a cooperation agreement on the peaceful use of nuclear energy.

Toward the end of 1985, Premier Zhao Ziyang paid a visit to Argentina, Brazil, Colombia, and Venezuela and announced a series of principles for enhancing relations between China and Latin America. The so-called Four Principles for Relations between China and Latin America were the following: (1) Peace and Friendship; (2) Mutual Support; (3) Equality and Mutual Benefit; and (4) the Search for Common Progress.[28] Later, in May 1988, President Raúl Alfonsín went to China and signed three cooperation agreements on aerospace, animal health, and Antarctic research matters.

After the 1989–91 events (the Tiananmen Square massacre and then the collapse of communism in eastern Europe and Russia), the PRC's domestic and international policies were strongly affected at both a national and an international level. On the domestic front, these events allowed the more conservative elements of the CCP to strengthen their positions, while on the international front, the country had to face sanctions imposed by the West. This situation, and the simultaneous evolution of a unipolar world, encouraged Beijing to implement a campaign to overcome its strategic and diplomatic isolation.

High-level visits, which had become less frequent during those years, were restored. In May 1990, President Yang Shangkun made an official visit to the Americas from north to south. The Chinese head of state visited Mexico, Brazil, Uruguay, Argentina, and Chile and took the opportunity to underscore matters of common interest to both regions, such as opposition to hegemonism, respect for the principle of nonintervention in domestic affairs of other countries, and the establishment of a new international economic order. In November of that same year, Argentine president Carlos S. Menem returned Yang's visit and stayed in Beijing for four days.

In 1993, Chinese foreign affairs minister Qian Qichen paid an official visit to Argentina. In 1994, the president of the People's National Assembly, Qiao Shi, visited Argentina and Brazil, and during his stay he once again expressed China's solidarity regarding the establishment of a new international economic order. He also endorsed Argentina's claim to sovereignty over the Malvinas Islands.[29] Later, in 1995, the Argentine head of state paid his second official visit to the PRC.

The Economic Dimension of Argentina-China Relations

China is the largest Asian buyer of Argentine goods.[30] Economic relations between the two countries have developed impressively because of reciprocal interests. The regularity with which the meetings of the Commission on Trade and Economic Cooperation were held illustrates the shared interest in dealing with different aspects of economic cooperation and overcoming existing barriers.

Economic cooperation agreements have been gradually adapted to economic openness processes in Argentina and the PRC. These have allowed, among other aspects, the use of maritime transport, the establishment of binational Chinese-Argentine companies, and the reciprocal protection of investments. A considerable number of Chinese enterprises have permanent representations in Argentina, and vice versa. They mainly operate in areas such as oil operation, port infrastructure, and hydroelectric power machinery. Chinese investment in Argentina has mainly focused on the chemical (fertilizers), fishing, and electronics industries.

In the foreign trade sphere, Argentine exports to China have shown significant growth since 1992, increasing from US$130 million to US$870 million, especially during 1996, when sales to the PRC soared at a rate of over 110 percent. During that same period, Chinese imports into Argentina increased from US$480 million to US$1.1 billion, respectively. The trade balance for this period showed a deficit for Argentina estimated at around US$2.3 billion. In 2001, global trade with China, considering Asian-Pacific countries, ranked second; if one considers only Argentine exports, then China becomes Argentina's main trading partner. The main products sold by Argentina to China include seeds and oleaginous fruit (32 percent of the total amount), fat, and animal and vegetable oils (28 percent), furs and leathers (14.3 percent), and prepared pet food (7 percent). Argentina's main imports from China are machinery, spare parts, and electronic devices and appliances (21 percent of total amount); boilers and mechanical devices (16 percent); toys (9 percent); and organic chemical products (8 percent).

President Kirchner's June 2004 visit to Beijing aimed to further consolidate the growing trade relationship. Chinese and Argentine leaders agreed to expand cooperative efforts in the arenas of communications, sea transport, lumber processing, energy, and raw materials in addition to the keystone field of agriculture. In 2003, Sino-Argentine trade reached $3.18 billion, up an impressive 123 percent from 2002.[31]

Prospects for Future Argentine-PRC Relations

This analysis of Argentine-PRC relations suggests a historical continuum that, though not long in duration, is developing successfully. This has manifested itself in ever-expanding diplomatic, political, economic, and cultural relations between the two countries.

Political ties, despite geographical and cultural distances, can be considered normal. Gestures of friendship have formed a continuing characteristic of ties between Argentina and China. These gestures have translated into material aid measures, mutual respect, and sympathy for each other's situation, such as China's support of Argentina's position during the Malvinas conflict with Great Britain.

It is possible to believe that, in the international system built since the end of the Cold War, political ties between Argentina and China could become even stronger. This may come about by virtue of the transformation of power in the Asia-Pacific region from the 1990s onward, which has meant, for some, a persistent loss of relative power (both political and economic), and for China, a sustained growth in diplomatic, material, and military strength.

China's rise creates a special opportunity for Buenos Aires, especially at a time when Argentina has been forced to diversify its political and economic relations internationally due to the difficulties and isolation it is undergoing. Regarding trade, it is important to recognize the low percentage of Argentine sales to China within the context of Argentina's exports to the rest of the world, as well as the fact that over 60 percent of these sales are based on raw materials or have very little added value coming from four basic categories: grain-based pet food; fat, and animal and vegetable oils; seeds and ole-aginous fruits; and minerals, slag, and ashes. Argentine imports from China have soared during recent years, showing an increase of over 300 percent.

Argentine food products have greater advantages in the Chinese market because con-sumer needs in this area are significant. This can be attributed to a strong current trend toward adopting consumption patterns involving highly varied products and the westernization of Chinese consumer culture. This is, in turn, reinforced by the stability of markets in the Asia-Pacific region (after the 1997 Asian crisis), and as a result of this, a significant development of Argentina's relations with that entire region is expected to take place in the years to come.

We must also consider the Asia-Pacific region's interest in Argentina because of its po-litical role in Latin America, as well as its rich human and natural resources. At the same time, Buenos Aires must adopt a series of measures to make Argentina also recog-nized for its seriousness, its respect for the so-called rules of the game, its responsible entrepreneurial practices, and its improved understanding of other cultures.

In brief, although political and economic contacts have been successful so far, evolution to a "grand policy" level and expanded impact on broader Argentine society (outside govern-ment) have yet to materialize. This new century presents a challenge for public and private-sector decision makers from both parties. The continuation and fruitful development of bilateral relations require a considerable amount of knowledge about each other's respec-tive national conditions, as well as creativity and courage to realize bilateral potential.

Conclusion

Chinese activities in Latin America are neither large-scale nor threatening. Beijing's central goal in Latin America is to find new markets for its wide array of exports, as well as to tap the region's resources for China's development. Enhanced relations with states in Latin America are additionally intended to support China's broader goals of multipolarization and to diplomatically isolate Taiwan. But there appears to be no Chi-nese appetite for challenging the United States in what China regards as a U.S. sphere of strong influence. Other PRC goals in Latin America include gaining access to both Western technology and business practices, supporting ethnic Chinese communities while avoiding any associations with international criminal organizations, acquiring raw materials and foodstuffs, and improving its international image.

China is gradually returning to the international scene, having transformed itself into a genuine great power. This is a new element within the global order that deserves care-ful analysis. Emerging powers have many times in the past been aggressive and brutal as they sought to achieve their "place in the sun." Furthermore, they have mistrusted their competitors, taking advantage of every possible chance to weaken potential adversaries.

The direction that Chinese civilization may adopt in this new century will have an important impact on the international system in the coming years. China will continue to influence neighboring countries in Asia, but inevitably it will also seek to expand this influence to the rest of the world as its economy grows.

As Robert D. Kaplan observes, future relations with China will entail the exercise of a "realpolitik," which should be unsentimental and based on a true scholarly understanding of its idiosyncrasies.[32] Yet it would be extremely premature to react hysterically to the rise of China.

Although in the past Beijing focused its utmost attention on relations with Washington and Moscow, today China has built strong links to the rest of the international community. Latin America will be a part of that agenda. In the last decades, Chinese authorities have perceived that their neighboring countries were relatively stable and did not offer significant strategic difficulties. Within this encouraging context, China has started to develop sound political and economic ties with Latin American nations.

It is to be expected that the PRC will continue to prioritize its national security and development. Therefore, it will be especially alert to events pertaining to the United States, Russia, and the affairs of East Asia generally. However, China will also pay attention to those countries that can help develop its economy. Although there is a very low probability of significant capital investment in the coming years, there is a significant possibility of technology transfer in many areas. China's trend toward diversifying technology sources will foster trade with this region. Each side will also seek to work with the other to complement their trade development policies and offset protectionist measures taken in other important markets in Europe and North America.

From a national-security perspective, the most important areas to watch within contemporary PRC relations with Latin America include Sino-Brazilian aerospace cooperation, Chinese influence in the Panama Canal region, and Sino-Cuban military and intelligence ties. While none of these issues represents a concrete threat to hemispheric security in the forseeable future, this benign assessment could require modification as Asia-Pacific security in the twenty-first century continues to evolve.

Notes

1. See David Shambaugh, *Modernizing China's Military: Progress, Problems and Prospects* (London: University of California Press, 2002), pp. 125, 129.

2. Ying Ma, "China's America Problem," *Policy Review,* no. 111 (February 2002), p. 2.

3. Sun Tzu, *The Art of War* (Madrid: Denma, 2001), pp. 44–47.

4. *2000 Annual Report on the Military Power of the People's Republic of China, Report to Congress Pursuant to the FY 2000 National Defense Authorization Act* (Washington, D.C.: U.S. Department of Defense, 2000), pp. 5–6.

5. Yong Deng, "Hegemon on the Offensive: Chinese Perspectives on U.S. Global Strategy," *Political Science Quarterly* 116, no. 3 (Fall 2001), p. 355.

6. Ibid., p. 359.

7. Randall L. Schweller, "New Realistic Research on Alliances," *American Political Science Review* 91 (December 1997), p. 929.

8. Recognizing this problem, China recently unveiled a new initiative to redevelop the northeast. The challenge is daunting.

9. "China's 21st Century Africa Policy Evolving," Stratfor.com, 7 August 2002.

10. Xin Zan and Bian Yi, "Ducaizhe Xuexiao" (School for Autocrats), *Guoji Zhanwang* (World Outlook), January 2002, pp. 80–83.

11. Hong Yuyi, *Lamei Guoji Guanxi Shigang* (A Historical Survey of the International Relations of Latin America) (Beijing: Waiyu Jiaoxue Yu Yanjiu Chubanshe, 1996), pp. 1, 502.

12. Data in this paragraph are drawn from Geraldo Samor and Joel Millman, "Brazil Seeks to Broaden China Trade," *Wall Street Journal,* 21 May 2004.

13. Data in this paragraph are from Todd Benson, "China Fuels Brazil's Dream of Being a Steel Power," *New York Times,* 21 May 2004.

14. Bernard D. Cole, *Oil for the Lamps of China—Beijing's 21st Century Search for Energy,* McNair Paper No. 67 (Washington, D.C.: National Defense University, 2003), pp. 15–16.

15. See, for example, Adam Easton, "Venezuela Backs China in Plane Row," *BBC News,* 17 April 2001, available at news.bbc.co.uk/1/hi/world/americas/1280995.stm.

16. Xu Shicheng, director of the research department of the Institute for Latin American Studies, Chinese Social Sciences Academy, and secretary general of the Chinese Association for Latin American Studies (presentation to Ninth Financial and Banking Seminar on the Perspectives of Political and Economic Relations between the People's Republic of China and Latin America, 11th plenary session, Buenos Aires, 1 April 1999).

17. Ko-Lin Chin, *Smuggled Chinese: Clandestine Immigration to the United States* (Philadelphia: Temple University Press, 1999), p. 49.

18. Jennifer Bolz, "Chinese Organized Crime and Illegal Alien Trafficking: Human and Commodity," *Asian Affairs* 22, no. 3 (Fall 95), p. 147.

19. "The South American Banking System," *Taipei Today* 18, no. 2 (March–April 1999).

20. "Challenges to Security and Crimes of the XXI Century," *Proceedings of the XIV Frontier Seminar* (Buenos Aires: Escuela Superior de Gendarmería, 1996), pp 13–16.

21. "Alleged Mafia Lord to Be Indicted for Tax Evasion," *ABC* (Paraguay), 17 September 2001.

22. "Chinese Origin Residents Detained and Questioned Regarding Possible Link to Mafia," *Noticias* (Paraguay), 26 October 2001.

23. Roberto Godoy, "Triple Border Area Monitored during the Past 20 Years," *O Estado de São Paolo,* 11 November 2001.

24. "Russia Warily Finesses China Ties," Stratfor.com, 24 July 2002, available at www.cdi.org/russia/216-10.cfm. This analyst contends that these rumors are intended by Moscow to fuel Sino-American antagonism, which Russia may view as consistent with its national interests.

25. See, for example, "China Provides Cuba with Logistic Items, Not Arms," 14 June 2001, available at www.intellnet.org/resources/pacom_ep3_homepage/eng/.

26. Dale Eisman, "Realignment of Navy Ships Likely to Affect Bases in Pacific Region," *Norfolk Virginian-Pilot,* 25 June 2003.

27. Li He, *Sino-Latin American Economic Relations* (New York: Praeger, 1991), pp. 53–54.

28. "Premier Zhao Announces the Four Principles for Sino-Latin American Relations," *Beijing Informa,* no. 46 (November 1985), p. 3.

29. "Report on President Yang's Official Visit to Latin America," *Renmin Ribao,* 17 November 1994, p. 2.

30. The literature employed to assess this subject comes from interviews and statistics graciously provided by the deactivated Analysis Unit for Asian-Pacific Matters of the Ministry of Economy and by the International Economic Negotiations Undersecretariat of the Argentine Foreign Affairs Ministry.

31. "Huge Potential in Argentina-China Trade," *Xinhua,* 29 June 2004, available at china.org.cn/english/international/99642.htm.

32. Robert D. Kaplan, "China: A World Power Again," *Atlantic Monthly* 284, no. 2 (August 1999), pp. 16–18.

Conclusion

Read together, the three studies included in this volume paint a picture of real and immediate threats to the security interests of Latin American countries and the United States. They suggest, at least implicitly, that countries north and south of the Rio Grande have much to gain from working together to meet those challenges. Even a cursory review of the current dynamic in the Western Hemisphere could lead to a conclusion that not enough dialogue on security is taking place, much less the kind of concerted action required to address the threats. A review of some of the main findings included in the preceding chapters may both offer an explanation for what is wrong with this picture and suggest a way forward.

In their analysis of "new threats" in Latin America's lawless areas and failed states, Cirino, Elizondo, and Wawro conclude that the terrorist menace breeds in the slums and ungoverned areas of Latin America. It is inseparable from the economic, social, and political problems of the region. Terrorist basing is possible in all of the victim and accomplice states, as well as in the "lawless areas" described in their chapter. They suggest a two-tracked approach to addressing the security threats they identify. First, every effort must be made to penetrate, expose, and destroy terrorist cells, and their links to drug production and sales. Further, the authors advocate a "kind of subtle nation-building" aimed at eliminating the conditions that support terrorists and *narcos,* as well as fervently anti-American "populist movements." While ascribing high salience to a terrorist threat in Latin America, they explicitly conclude that Islamic terrorism is a minor concern for the region.

In a complementary analysis, Taylor looks specifically at recent poor economic performance in the major economies of Latin America and finds adverse security consequences flowing from the short-term economic situation. Even though a sluggish world economy was a major contributor to poor growth rates in Latin America at the beginning of this decade, publics in the region understandably associated their distress with their own democratically elected governments and the market-oriented policy

reforms adopted during the previous decade. A consequent decline in support for democracy erodes the potential for stable, responsive government that promises a new
era of social peace. At the same time, in several countries, rising crime rates and civil
unrest flowed directly from economic hardship. The potential for international or domestic terrorists to exploit this situation echoes the conclusions of the first chapter. To
the extent that Latin Americans saw the United States as responsible for their economic
plight, either because it was preoccupied with wars in Afghanistan and Iraq or because
it was identified with the unpopular policy reforms associated with the Washington
Consensus, relations with the United States were harmed and security cooperation was
complicated. Looking beyond the short term, Taylor also sees security problems ema-
nating from the highly inequitable distribution of income prevalent in Latin America.
As with short-term economic distress, one finds a high correlation between this form of
economic injustice and lack of support for democracy and heightened rates of crime.

The chapter by Delamer, Goldstein, Malena, and Porn has a different point of departure from the first two: it asks whether the rising power of China, an external state,
poses an emerging threat in the Latin American region. The authors identify three security issues of concern. The first relates to the presence of the Panama Ports Company, a subsidiary of the Hong Kong–based company Hutchison Whampoa Limited,
to operate access ports on either end of the Panama Canal. Their examination of the
evidence leads them to a tentative conclusion that this investment is unlikely to become a decisive factor in any U.S.-China maritime conflict scenario. The other security issues they address relate to the foci of the other two chapters in this volume:
"triads" and illegal immigration. The activities of the "triads," tightly structured organizations for carrying out transnational crime, include money laundering and illegal
immigration. While currently aimed at resettling Chinese nationals abroad, this immigration network might be exploited by international terrorist groups with a political/
military agenda.

Can we see any pattern in the nature of the security threats treated in this volume?
First, one can be identified as *sui generis:* the Hutchison Whampoa investments at the
Atlantic and Pacific ends of the Panama Canal. Although the researchers who evaluate
that phenomenon downplay its security significance, had it been deemed to pose a serious threat, it could have been categorized as a threat from a foreign state, given the relationship between the Chinese government and investors based in China.

All the other threats included in the three essays share certain characteristics. Whether
they are domestic or transnational, the significant actors are not states. They do not re-
semble military threats in their equipment, technology, or force structure; nor are

military means uniquely appropriate to respond to them, even though effective counters may include a military component. More often, what is needed is a combination of law enforcement and intelligence operations to address the symptoms, and economic and social programs to meet the underlying causes of the threats.

The authors recognize that the selection of topics for the chapters in this volume could not include all the important security issues in the Americas today. They are confident, though, that the present topics are among the most important, even in countries of Latin America that have not been singled out for extensive treatment here. The most notable omission is full attention to the narco-terrorist threat in Colombia.[1]

One can be heartened by the realization that the problems treated here as security threats are widely perceived as such. Indeed, the *Declaration on Security in the Americas,* adopted by the Special Conference on Security of the Organization of American States in October 2003 in Mexico City, included a reference to all of them, plus some others:

> The security of states of the hemisphere is affected, in different ways, by the traditional threats and the following new threats, concerns, and other challenges of a diverse nature:
>
> - Terrorism, transnational organized crime, the global drug problem, corruption, asset laundering, illicit trafficking in weapons, and the connections among them.
>
> - Extreme poverty and social exclusion of broad sectors of the population, which also affect stability and democracy. Extreme poverty erodes social cohesion and undermines the security of states.
>
> - Natural and man-made disasters, HIV/AIDS and other diseases, other health risks, and environmental degradation.
>
> - Trafficking in persons.
>
> - Attacks to cyber security.
>
> - The potential for damage in the event of an accident or incident during the maritime transport of potentially hazardous materials, including petroleum and radioactive materials and toxic waste.
>
> - The possibility of terrorist access, possession, and use of weapons of mass destruction and their means of delivery.[2]

What the *Declaration on Security* masked, though, in its catchall statement of the diplomatic consensus that was possible in Mexico City was the different emphases given by different countries of the Americas to specific threats. But for this factor, it ought to be easy to reach agreement on working together, north and south, on solutions. In fact, a review of statements by leaders of the major countries in North and South America illustrates a lack of consensus on the priorities that should be attached to the security threats (see table 1).

TABLE 1
Intensities of Governments' Perceptions of Threats

	UNITED STATES	LATIN AMERICA*
State-to-State Threat	Moderate	Low
International Terrorist Threat	**High**	**Moderate**
Threat to Economic Security	**Moderate**	**High**
Threat of Domestic Violence	Low	Moderate

*Cuba and Venezuela are excluded here because statements by Fidel Castro and Hugo Chávez indicate that they perceive a moderate-to-high state threat to their countries' security.

Achieving a shared threat assessment is key to cooperation, because if countries do not share a common perception of a threat, it will be difficult at best for them to work together to meet it. Thus, in the most prominent recent case of action to counter a putative state threat, the governments of Mexico and Chile were unwilling as members of the UN Security Council to support the position of the United States that another resolution should be passed to authorize the use of force against Iraq. At the other end of the spectrum arrayed above, the threat of domestic violence does not pose the same challenge to the government of the United States as, say, urban challenges may in Brazil or ethnic unrest in Peru, Bolivia, or Ecuador.

There seems, though, to be more consensus between Washington and Latin American capitals on terrorism and economic challenges. Certainly in Colombia, the narco-terrorist nexus presents a clear danger to Colombian stability and institutions, while the narcotics it produces endanger public health in the United States. To the extent that foreign terrorists aid and abet their Colombian counterparts, the shared threat perception is strengthened further. The U.S. trade representative, Robert B. Zoellick, has often made the case that freer trade, by leading to greater prosperity and closer ties among trading countries, promotes security.[3]

If it were possible to craft the modest consensus on the highlighted items in table 1 into a sort of grand bargain on hemispheric security and economic progress, Latin American countries and the United States might find it easier to cooperate to satisfy their security objectives. One of the biggest challenges, oddly enough, may be bureaucratic barriers *within* governments. Since September 11, we have gained a new appreciation of the difficulty of forging cooperation among agencies responsible for one aspect or another of national security. The kind of comprehensive approach called for here requires communication and cooperation not only among the broad range of security institutions but, in addition, with those agencies also responsible for economic and commercial policy.

Difficult as implementing this program may be, it could be the best way available to get the high degree of engagement among the governments of the Americas that is required to improve security throughout the hemisphere.

Notes

1. An important contribution to understanding the conflict in Colombia is available in a recent series of monographs published by the Strategic Studies Institute of the U.S. Army War College.

2. Organization of American States, *Declaration on Security in the Americas* (Mexico City, Mexico: Special Conference on Security, October 27–28, 2003), p. 4.

3. See, e.g., Office of the U.S. Trade Representative, Identification of Trade Expansion Priorities Pursuant to Executive Order 13116, April 30, 2001.

Bibliography

LEGAL MATERIALS

Sentencia Juez Antonio Veloso Pelejero [Sentence by Judge Antonio Veloso Pelejero]. Proceso 1015/2000, p. 1. (Poder Judicial, Estado de Mato Grosso, 13 January 2003.)

PRINT SOURCES

"Arequipa's Anger, Peru's Problem." *The Economist,* 22 June 2002, p. 33.

"Challenges to Security and Crimes of the XXI Century." *Proceedings of the XIV Frontier Seminar,* pp. 13–16. Buenos Aires: Escuela Superior de Gendarmería, 1996.

"A Decline Without Parallel." *The Economist,* 2 March 2002, p. 26.

"Guerrillas—or Terrorists?" *The Economist,* 8 December 2001.

"Islamist Terrorism in Latin America." *Jane's Terrorism and Security Monitor,* 1 October 2003.

"The Longest Journey: A Survey of Migration." *The Economist,* 2 November 2002, p. 6.

"Opening the Door." *The Economist,* 2 November 2002, p. 11.

"The South American Banking System." *Taipei Today* 18, no. 2 (March–April 1999).

"The Stubborn Survival of Frustrated Democrats." *The Economist,* 1 November 2003, p. 33.

"Superman Uribe Holds Back the Tide." *The Economist,* 7 June 2003, p. 30.

Andreas, Peter. "Smuggling Wars: Law Enforcement and Law Evasion in a Changing World." *Transnational Crime in the Americas: An Inter-American Dialogue Book,* ed. Thomas Farer, pp. 85–99. New York: Routledge, 1999.

Bartolome, Mariano Cesar. "La Triple Frontera: Principal Foco de Inseguridad en el Cono Sur Americano [The Triple Frontier: Principal Focus of Insecurity in the South American Cone]." *Military Review* 82, no. 4 (July–August 2002).

Benavente Urbina, Andrés. "Rupturismo Social y Vulnerabilidad de las Instituciones en America Latina [Social Rupture and the Vulnerability to Latin American Institutions]." Paper presented to the Conference on Building Regional Security in the Western Hemisphere, Miami, Fla., 2–4 March 2003.

Bender, Bryan. "Visible Cracks: Narco-Terrorism in Colombia." *Jane's Defence Weekly* 40, no. 3 (9 July 2003).

Bitencourt, Luis. "Brazil's Growing Insecurity: Is It a Threat to Brazilian Democracy?" *Policy Papers on the Americas* 14, no. 1. Washington, D.C.: Center for Strategic and International Studies, 2003.

Bobbio, Norberto. *Estado, gobierno y sociedad* [State, Government and Society]. Buenos Aires: Fondo de Cultura Económica, 2001.

Bolz, Jennifer. "Chinese Organized Crime and Illegal Alien Trafficking: Human and Commodity." *Asian Affairs: An American Review* 22, no. 3 (Fall 1995), pp. 147–59.

Brodie, Bernard. *War and Politics.* New York: Macmillan; London: Collier Macmillan, 1973.

Brzezinski, Matthew. "Re-engineering the Drug Business." *New York Times Magazine,* 23 June 2002, pp. 24–29, 46, 54–55.

Chin, Ko-Lin. *Smuggled Chinese: Clandestine Immigration to the United States.* Philadelphia: Temple University Press, 1999.

Deng, Yong. "Hegemon on the Offensive: Chinese Perspectives on U.S. Global Strategy." *Political Science Quarterly* 116, no. 3 (Fall 2001), pp. 343–65.

Diaz, Miguel, et al. "An Assessment of the Current Venezuelan Situation and Recommendations for the Future." *Policy Papers on the Americas* 12, no. 6. Washington, D.C.: Center for Strategic and International Studies, July 2002.

Dobriansky, Paula J. "Remarks to the 35th Annual Meeting and 2002 Forecast on Latin America and the Caribbean." Association of American Chambers of Commerce in Latin America, Washington, D.C., 8 May 2002.

Fajnzylber, Pablo, Daniel Lederman, and Norman Loayza. "Inequality and Violent Crime." *Journal of Law and Economics* 45, no. 1 (April 2002), pp. 1–40.

Farnan, Arie. "Colombia's Civil War Drifts South into Ecuador." *Christian Science Monitor,* 11 August 2002.

Godoy, Roberto. "Triple Border Area Monitored during the Past 20 Years." *O Estado de São Paolo,* 11 November 2001.

Goldberg, Jeffrey. "In the Party of God: Hezbollah Sets Up Operations in South America and the U.S." *New Yorker,* 28 October 2002, pp. 74–83.

Gomez Buendia, Hernando. "Security: Will We See Results?" *Semana,* 13–19 January 2003.

Graf Lambsdorff, Johann. "2002 Corruption Perceptions Index." *Global Corruption Report: Covering Worldwide Corruption from July 2001 to June 2002,* pp. 262–65. Berlin: Transparency International, 28 August 2002.

Guillermoprieto, Alma. "Letter from Colombia: Waiting for War." *New Yorker,* 13 May 2002, pp. 48–55.

Gurr, Ted Robert. *Why Men Rebel.* Princeton, N.J.: Princeton Univ. Press, 1970.

He, Li. *Sino-Latin American Economic Relations.* New York: Praeger, 1991.

Helman, Gerald B., and Steven R. Ratner. "Saving Failed States." *Foreign Policy,* no. 89 (Winter 1993), pp. 3–21.

Hudson, Peter. "There Are No Terrorists Here: Hezbollah Activities in South America." *Newsweek International,* 19 November 2001, pp. 39–42.

International Organization for Migration. "Trafficking in Migrants: Some Global and Regional Perspectives." Paper submitted to the Regional Conference on Migrations, Puebla, Mexico, 13–14 March 1996.

Kaplan, Robert D. "China: A World Power Again." *Atlantic Monthly* 284, no. 2 (August 1999), pp. 16–18.

Kawell, JoAnn. "Terror's Latin American Profile." *NACLA Report on the Americas* 35, no. 3 (November–December 2001), pp. 50–53.

Kennedy, Paul. *The Rise and Fall of the Great Powers.* New York: Vintage House, 1987.

Rairan, Juan A. "Colombian Narcoterrorism's Strategic Implications." Unpublished paper, U.S. Naval War College, Newport, R.I., May 2003.

Reis, Fábio Wanderley. "Atualidade Mundial e Desafios Brasileiros [Current World and Brazilian Challenges]." *Estudos Avançados* 14, no. 39 (May–August 2000), pp. 14–20.

Riffle, Conor. "Welcome to Argentina, Mr. Kirchner." *Council on Hemispheric Affairs,* 3 June 2003.

Robinson, Linda. Remarks at Pell Center. Newport, R.I., 1 December 2000.

———. "Terror Close to Home." *U.S. News & World Report,* 6 October 2003, pp. 20–22, 24.

Rotberg, Robert. "Failed States in a World of Terror." *Foreign Affairs* 81, no. 4 (July–August 2002), pp. 127–40.

———. "The New Nature of Nation-State Failure." *Washington Quarterly* 25, no. 3 (Summer 2002), pp. 85–96.

Santos Rubino, Alejandro. "Semana Director on Colombia's Inability to Resolve Social Crisis." *Semana,* 3–9 February 2002.

Schweller, Randall L. "New Realistic Research on Alliances." *American Political Science Review* 91, no. 4 (December 1997), pp. 927–30.

Shambaugh, David. *Modernizing China's Military: Progress, Problems and Prospects.* London: University of California Press, 2002.

Shicheng, Xu. "The Perspectives of Political and Economic Relations between the People's Republic of China and Latin America." Presentation to the Ninth Financial and Banking Seminar, 11th plenary session, Buenos Aires, 1 April 1999.

Solimano, Andrés. *Remittances by Emigrants: Issues and Evidence.* Santiago: Economic Commission for Latin America and the Caribbean, 2003.

Sun, Tzu. *The Art of War.* Madrid: Denma, 2001.

United Nations. Economic Commission for Latin America and the Caribbean [hereafter ECLAC]. "Almost Twenty Million Latinamericans and Caribbeans Are Migrants." Press release, 20 November 2002.

———. *Globalization and Development,* LC/ G.2157 (SES.29/3). Brasilia, Brazil, 6–10 May 2002.

Van Dongen, Rachel. "The Right Man." *New Republic,* 16 June 2003, pp. 12–13.

Williamson, John, ed. *Latin American Adjustment: How Much Has Happened?* Washington, D.C.: Institute for International Economics, 1990.

Woodward, Susan. "Failed States: Warlordism and 'Tribal' Warfare." *Naval War College Review* 52, no. 2 (Spring 1999), pp. 55–68. Zan, Xin, and Bian Yi. "Ducaizhe Xuexiao [School for Autocrats]." *Guoji Zhanwang* (World Outlook), January 2002, pp. 80–83.

ONLINE SOURCES

FBIS. "Argentine Army Chief Opposes Military Involvement in Domestic Security Matters." *Pagina 12*, 7 May 2003.

———. "Brazil: Defense Minister Viegas Discusses Shoot-down Law, FARC Activities." *Brasilia Air Force Command*, 20 May 2003.

———. "Brazilian Defense Minister's Views on Role of Armed Forces." *O Estado de São Paolo*, 13 January 2003.

"China Provides Cuba with Logistic Items, Not Arms." 14 June 2001. www.china-embassy.org/eng/12862.html, and www.intellnet.org/resources/pacom_ep3_homepage/eng.

"Defence Market Latin America." *Armada International* 27, no. 2 (April–May 2003). www.armada.ch/03-2/complete_03-2.pdf (accessed 22 April 2004).

"Evo Morales: 'no habrá alianzas.'" *BBCMundo.com*, 27 June 2002. news.bbc.co.uk/hi/spanish/specials/elecciones_en_bolivia/newsid_2070000/2070135.stm (accessed 22 April 2004).

"Russia Warily Finesses China Ties." *Stratfor*, 24 July 2002. www.cdi.org/russia/216-10.cfm (accessed 22 April 2004).

Acosta Silva, Adrián. "Gobernabilidad y Democracia: Perspectivas del Debate a Veinte Años del Reporte a la Comisión Trilateral [Governability and Democracy: Perspectives on Twenty Years of Debate on the Report to the Trilateral Commission]." *Nóesis* 13 (July–December 1994). www.uacj.mx/Publicaciones/noesis/adrian.htm (accessed 22 April 2004).

Andersen, Martin Edwin. "Al-Qaeda across the Americas." *Insight on the News*, 26 November 2001. www.insightmag.com/news/2001/11/26/World/AlQaeda.Across.The.Americas-138421.shtml (accessed 22 April 2004).

Brana-Shute, Gary. "Narco Criminality in the Caribbean: Global Problems in Small Places." Talk at Georgetown University, Washington, D.C., 2000. www.trinitydc.edu/academics/depts/Interdisc/International/caribbean%20briefings/Caribbean%20Paper %20Series.pdf (accessed 22 April 2004).

Brandao, Marcia, and Carla Benevides. "U.S. Retaliation Jeopardizes Amazon Surveillance." *Brazilian Camara dos Deputados*, 30 April 2003 (FBIS).

Center for Strategic and International Studies. "Hemisphere Highlights: Americas Program." 2, no. 6 (June 2003). csis.org/americas/pubs/hh/0306.pdf (accessed 22 April 2004).

Constance, Paul. "Secrecy Is a Form of Corruption." *IDB America*, March 2001. www.iadb.org/idbamerica/English/FEB01E/feb01e11.html (accessed 22 April 2004).

Ghersi, Enrique. "South America's New Style Military Coup." *Christian Science Monitor*, 19 June 2003. www.csmonitor.com/2003/0619/p11s02-coop.html (accessed 22 April 2004).

Inter-American Development Bank. *Facing Up to Inequality in Latin America: Economic and Social Progress in Latin America, 1998–1999 Report*. September 1999. www.iadb.org/res/index.cfm?fuseaction=Publications.View&pub_id=B-1998-1999 (accessed 22 April 2004).

———. "IDB Study Warns of Disillusionment with Democracy." 9 March 2002. www.iadb.org/exr/PRENSA/2002/cp5602E.htm (accessed 22 April 2004).

Inter-American Dialogue. *The Troubled Americas*. Policy Report 2003. Washington, D.C.: Inter-American Dialogue Publications, 2003. www.iadialog.org/publications/policy_reports/PlenaryReport03.pdf (accessed 20 April 2004).

Lesmes, Jorge. "Colombian Military Leaders Proclaim Guerrillas' Defeat." *El Espectador* (Bogotá), 4 May 2003 (FBIS).

Lopez, Vladimir. "Nicaraguan Foreign Ministry Reacts to OAS Report on Diversion of Weapons." *El Nuevo Diario* (Managua), 21 January 2003 (FBIS).

Luiz, Edson. "Brazil Steps Up Security to Fight Organized Crime on Border." *O Estado de São Paolo*, 28 April 2003 (FBIS).

Ma, Ying. "China's America Problem." *Policy Review*, no. 111 (February–March 2002). www.policyreview.org/FEB02/ma.html (accessed 22 April 2004).

Marcella, Gabriel. *The U.S. and Colombia: The Journey from Ambiguity to Strategic Clarity*. Strategic Studies Institute monograph, U.S. Army War College, Carlisle, PA, May 2003. www.carlisle.army.mil/ssi/pubs/2003/journey/journey.htm (accessed 22 April 2004).

Mendel, William W. "Paraguay's Ciudad del Este and the New Centers of Gravity." *Military Review* 82, no. 2 (March–April 2002). fmso.leavenworth.army.mil/FMSOPUBS/ ISSUES/paraguay/paraguay.htm (accessed 22 April 2004).

Metz, Steven. *The Future of Insurgency.* Strategic Studies Institute monograph, U.S. Army War College, Carlisle, PA, December 1993. www.carlisle.army.mil/ssi/pubs/1993/insurg/ insurg.htm (accessed 22 April 2004).

Millett, Richard L. *Colombia's Conflicts: the Spillover Effects of a Wider War.* Strategic Studies Institute monograph, U.S. Army War College, Carlisle, PA, October 2002. www.carlisle.army.mil/ssi/pubs/2002/colomcon/ colomcon.htm (accessed 22 April 2004).

Nagle, Luz E. *Plan Colombia: Reality of the Colombian Crisis and Implications for Hemispheric Security.* Strategic Studies Institute monograph, U.S. Army War College, Carlisle, PA, October 2002. www.carlisle.army.mil/ssi/pubs/2002/ pcrealty/pcrealty.htm (accessed 22 April 2004).

Naim, Moises. "Fads and Fashion in Economic Reforms: Washington Consensus or Washington Confusion?" Remarks at International Conference on Second Generation Reforms, Washington, D.C., 26 October 1999. www.imf.org/ external/pubs/ft/seminar/1999/reforms/ Naim.htm (accessed 22 April 2004).

Noriega, Roger F. "Traditional Threats, New Concerns, and Other Challenges to Hemispheric Security." Remarks at the Inter-American Defense College. Fort McNair, Washington, D.C., 22 October 2003. www.state.gov/p/wha/rls/rm/ 25753.htm (accessed 22 April 2004).

Nuñez, Joseph. *A 21st Century Security Architecture for the Americas: Multilateral Cooperation, Liberal Peace and Soft Power.* Strategic Studies Institute monograph, U.S. Army War College, Carlisle, PA, August 2000. www.carlisle.army .mil/ssi/pubs/2002/21cntury/21cntury.htm (accessed 22 April 2004).

Organization for Economic Cooperation and Development. *First Estimate for GDP in the OECD Area, Fourth Quarter of 2002.* Paris, 17 March 2003. www.oecd.org/document/13/0,2340,en _2649_34261_2500941_1_1_1_1,00.html (accessed 22 April 2004).

Powell, Colin L. Intervention at the Plenary of the General Assembly of the Organization of American States. Santiago, Chile, 9 June 2003.

www.state.gov/secretary/rm/2003/21330.htm (accessed 22 April 2004).

Ralston, Erin. "Evo Morales and Opposition to the U.S. in Bolivia." *ZNet Daily Commentaries,* 14 July 2002. www.zmag.org/sustainers/content/ 2002-07/14ralston.cfm (accessed 22 April 2004).

Rempe, Dennis P. *The Past as Prologue? A History of U.S. Counterinsurgency Policy in Colombia, 1958–1966.* Strategic Studies Institute monograph, U.S. Army War College, Carlisle, PA, March 2002. www.carlisle.army.mil/ssi/pubs/ 2002/past/past.htm (accessed 22 April 2004).

Rodrik, Dani. *Why Is There So Much Economic Insecurity in Latin America?* Paper prepared for the World Bank, October 1999. ksghome .harvard.edu/~.drodrik.academic.ksg/insecur .pdf (accessed 22 April 2004).

Rucker, Patrick. "Throughout the Americas, U.S. Increasingly Isolated Over Cuba." *Christian Science Monitor,* 12 June 2003. www.csmonitor.com/2003/0612/p07s01-woam .html (accessed 22 April 2004).

Rumsfeld, Donald H. "Statement by Secretary of Defense Donald H. Rumsfeld." Defense Ministerial of the Americas. Santiago, Chile, 19 November 2002. www.ciponline.org/colombia/ 02111904.htm (accessed 22 April 2004).

Santos Rubino, Alejandro. "Semana Director on Colombia's Inability to Resolve Social Crisis." *Semana,* 3–9 February 2002 (FBIS).

Schmidley, Dianne. *The Foreign-Born Population in the United States: March 2002.* Current Population Reports, P20-539. U.S. Census Bureau. Washington, D.C., 2003. www.census.gov/ prod/2003pubs/p20-539.pdf (accessed 22 April 2004).

Spanger, Hans-Joachim. "The Ambiguous Lessons of State Failure." Paper presented to the Failed States Conference, Florence, Italy, 10–14 April 2001. www.ippu.purdue.edu/failed_states/ 2001/papers/Spanger.pdf (accessed 22 April 2004).

United Nations. ECLAC. Unit on Investment and Corporate Strategies. *Foreign Direct Investment Flows into Latin America and the Caribbean, 2002 Report.* LC/G.2198-P/I. Santiago, Chile: ECLAC Publications, April 2003. www.eclac.cl/ publicaciones/DesarrolloProductivo/8/ LCG2198/ForeignInvestment2002.pdf (accessed 22 April 2004).

U.S. Department of Defense. *Annual Report on the Military Power of the People's Republic of China.* Report to Congress pursuant to the FY 2000 National Defense Authorization Act. Washington, D.C.: June 2000. www.defenselink.mil/news/Jun2000/china06222000.htm (accessed 22 April 2004).

Van Dongen, Rachel. "Colombian Rebels Abandon Arms." *Christian Science Monitor,* 28 May 2003. www.csmonitor.com/2003/0528/p06s02-woam.html (accessed 22 April 2004).

Verbitsky, Horacio. "Argentine Bill to Fight Terrorism." *Pagina 12,* 26 January 2003 (FBIS).

Whalen, Christopher. "Who is Protecting Hugo Chávez?" *Insight,* 25 November 2003 (FBIS).

The World Bank Group. Country Brief: Chile. lnweb18.worldbank.org/external/lac/lac.nsf/0/71BC8229DD493B2A85256C5A005D9093?OpenDocument (accessed 22 April 2004).

NEWSPAPERS

Arizona Daily Star, 5 November 2003.

Atlanta Journal-Constitution, 21 May 2003.

Baltimore Sun, 8 June 2003.

Beijing Informa, November 1985.

Brasilia Correio Braziliense (Brazil), 2 February 2003.

Chicago Tribune, 4 July 2003.

Daily Telegraph, 14 July 2003.

Dallas Morning News, 22 May 2003.

El Espectador (Bogotá), 11 May 2003.

Financial Times (UK), 23 April–15 November 2003.

Guoji Zhanwang [World Outlook] (PRC), January 2002.

International Herald Tribune, 12 May 2003.

Knight Ridder Newspapers, 22 January 2003.

London Sunday Telegraph, 9 November 2003.

Los Angeles Times, 24 May–8 November 2003.

Miami Herald, 7 April 2003–27 January 2004.

New York Times, 3 March 2002–23 November 2003.

Norfolk-Virginian Pilot, 25 June 2003.

Philadelphia Inquirer, 5 November 2003.

Renmin Ribao [People's Daily] (PRC), 17 November 1994.

San Diego Union-Tribune, 15 June 2003.

Semana (Colombia), 23 January 2003.

Taipei Today (Taiwan), March–April 1999.

Wall Street Journal, 4 February–1 July 2003.

Washington Post, 19 December 2002–5 January 2004.

Washington Times, 12 September 2002–29 December 2003.

TELEVISION AND ELECTRONIC NEWS SOURCES

ABC Color (Paraguay), 17 September 2001–30 January 2003.

Agence France Presse (Paris), 1 May 2003.

Agencia Centroamericana de Noticias (Panama), 23 January–25 April 2003.

BBC.co.uk, 2 June 2003.

Bogotá El Tiempo (Colombia).

Brasilia Correio Braziliense, 2 February 2003.

CNN.com.

El Correo (Lima), 2 May 2003.

LatinNews.com, 26 June 2003.

Madrid EFE, 4 May 2003.

Movimientobolivariano.org.

Noticias (Paraguay), 26 October 2001.

Pagina 12 (Argentina), 26 January–7 May 2003.

São Paolo Gazeta Mercantil, 5 May 2003.

Stratfor, 19 September 2001–4 September 2003.

ACANEFE (Panama), 23 January–25 April 2003.

Transparency.org.

Zmag.org, 14 July 2002.

Abbreviations

AUC	United Self-defenses of Colombia
CCP	Chinese Communist Party
CNP	Comprehensive National Power
CNWS	Center for Naval Warfare Studies of the U.S. Naval War College
CSIS	Center for Strategic and International Studies
ECLAC	Economic Commission for Latin America and the Caribbean of the United Nations
ELN	Army of National Liberation (Colombia)
ELN-B	Bolivian Army of National Liberation
FALG	Foreign Affairs Leadership Group
FARC	Revolutionary Armed Forces of Colombia
FBL	Bolivian Liberation Forces
FDI	Foreign Direct Investment
FTAA	Free Trade Area of the Americas
GDP	Gross Domestic Product
IDB	Inter-American Development Bank
ILEA	Institute for Latin American Studies, a member of the Chinese Social Sciences Academy
IMF	International Monetary Fund
NATO	North Atlantic Treaty Organization
OAS	Organization of American States
OECD	Organization for Economic Cooperation and Development
PLA	People's Liberation Army

PLAN	People's Liberation Army Navy
PPC	Panama Port Company
PRC	People's Republic of China
SARS	Severe Acute Respiratory Syndrome
SIVAM	Amazon Region Surveillance System
UNHRC	United Nations Human Rights Commission
WTO	World Trade Organization

Contributors

Julio A. Cirino is president of the Center for Hemispheric Studies Alexis de Tocqueville and a specialist in hemispheric security, defense, and international relations. He is also director of the Center for Conflict Studies of the University of Chile. Previously he held positions as adviser in the policy and strategy directorate of the Argentine Ministry of Defense and counselor in the Embassy of Argentina in Washington. He is a member of the International Institute of Strategic Studies in London, a correspondent of *Libertad Digital* of Madrid and *Radio Marti,* Miami, and an analyst of defense and security affairs for *CNN en español.*

Alberto R. Coll is chair of the Strategic Research Department and former Dean of Naval Warfare Studies at the U.S. Naval War College. He holds a B.A. from Princeton University and a J.D. and Ph.D. from the University of Virginia. From 1990 to 1993 he served as a Principal Deputy Assistant Secretary of Defense. He is the author of *The Wisdom of Statecraft* and has written widely on Latin American issues. This year he received Guatemala's Jose Antonio Irisarri Medal for his contributions to strengthening the rule of law, democratization, and civilian control of the military in that country. Dr. Coll is a member of the Council on Foreign Relations, the Virginia Bar, and the American Civil Liberties Union, and is a visiting professor at the Watson Institute of Brown University.

Guillermo R. Delamer is a member of the board of directors of the Center for Hemispheric Studies Alexis de Tocqueville, a private research institute, and a councillor at the Center for Strategic Studies of the Argentine Navy. He retired from the Argentine Navy as a rear admiral after a career aboard several types of surface ships that included three commands at sea. He is a graduate of the Naval Command College of the U.S. Naval War College and holds a master of science degree in management from Salve Regina University.

Silvana L. Elizondo is a director of the Center for Hemispheric Studies Alexis de Tocqueville and professor of history at the Belgrano University, Buenos Aires. Holder of a master's degree in international relations from Belgrano University, she also worked in defense and security studies at the *Universidad del Salvador,* Buenos Aires, and as institutional secretary of the *Fundación Integración.* She is a columnist and editor of *Agenda Internacional.*

Lyle J. Goldstein is associate professor of strategic studies and vice-director of the Eurasia Study Group at the U.S. Naval War College. He holds a B.A. from Harvard

University, an M.A. from the Nitze School of Advanced International Studies of Johns Hopkins University, and a Ph.D. from Princeton University. He has worked in the Office of the Secretary of Defense and at the Brookings Institution. He has lived and conducted extensive research in Russia and China and speaks both their languages fluently. His first book, *Preventive Attack and Weapons of Mass Destruction: A Comparative Historical Survey,* will be published by Stanford University Press in 2005.

Jorge Eduardo Malena teaches international relations and oriental studies at the Catholic University, Buenos Aires, and is an associate of the Center for Hemispheric Studies Alexis de Tocqueville and the Center for Strategic Studies of the Argentine Navy. He holds a bachelor's degree in political science and a master's degree in international relations from the Catholic University, Buenos Aires. He also earned a master of arts degree in Chinese area studies from the School of Oriental and African Studies of the University of London and is currently a Ph.D. candidate at the Catholic University, Buenos Aires.

Gabriela E. Porn serves as a research fellow at the Center for Hemispheric Studies Alexis de Tocqueville, a junior researcher at the Center for Strategic Studies of the Argentine Navy, and an analyst at the Argentine-Indian Chamber of Industry and Commerce. She is a graduate in political science of the Catholic University, Cordoba, and holds a master's degree in international relations from Belgrano University, Buenos Aires.

Paul D. Taylor is senior strategic researcher at the U.S. Naval War College, where he also teaches electives on Latin America and international economics and chaired the Latin American Studies Group. He holds an AB degree, *magna cum laude,* from Princeton University and a master's degree from Harvard University, where he studied economics. A former career Foreign Service officer, he served as U.S. ambassador to the Dominican Republic and deputy assistant secretary of state for Inter-American Affairs, and had four Latin American posts in which he lived and worked for periods of two to four years each. Before joining the Foreign Service, he served at sea as a naval officer.

Geoffrey Wawro is professor of strategic studies at the U.S. Naval War College. He holds a B.A., *magna cum laude,* from Brown University and a Ph.D. from Yale University. His books include *The Austro-Prussian War* (1996), *Warfare and Society in Europe, 1792–1914* (2000), and *The Franco-Prussian War* (2003), and he is North American editor of the *Cambridge Military Histories.* Wawro's scholarly articles and op-eds have been published in numerous academic journals and newspapers. He has appeared as a military analyst on Fox News Channel and is host and anchor of the History Channel's *Hard Target,* a weekly talk show with leading historians, statesmen, politicians, and journalists.

Collaborating Organizations

CENTER FOR NAVAL WARFARE STUDIES, U.S. NAVAL WAR COLLEGE
In 1981, almost a century after Stephen B. Luce founded the Naval War College as "a place of original research on all questions relating to war and to statesmanship connected with war, or the prevention of war," the Center for Naval Warfare Studies was established within the College as a nexus for broadly based, advanced research on the naval contribution to national strategy. The Center directly complements the curriculum of the Naval War College by providing a place for researching important professional issues which, in turn, inform and stimulate the faculty and students in the classroom. From its very beginning, the Center has linked the Naval War College to the fleet and policy makers in Washington by serving as a focal point, stimulus, and major source of strategic and campaign thought, by integrating strategic, campaign, and tactical concepts, by linking strategic concerns with technological developments, and, finally, by testing and evaluating concepts through war gaming.

Under the leadership and direction of the Dean of Naval Warfare Studies, a full-time, government-funded research staff works in six departments: Strategic Research, War Gaming, Advanced Research, Warfare Analysis and Research, Oceans Law and Policy, and the Naval War College Press, as well as a detachment of the Office of Naval Intelligence.

CENTER FOR STRATEGIC STUDIES OF THE ARGENTINE NAVY
The objective of the Center for Strategic Studies of the Argentine Navy is to constitute a center of studies and research aimed at expanding and deepening strategic understanding of national and international naval, maritime, and military issues in order to support decision making at the highest level of the Navy of Argentina. As part of its program, the Center also makes available to the broader society strategic analyses on national and international subjects related, especially, to maritime affairs.

The Center for Strategic Studies of the Argentine Navy, as an academic entity whose primary function is the analysis of national and international issues with special emphasis on military and maritime questions, works within the principle of academic freedom. While the Center is a direct dependency of the Office of the Argentine Chief of Naval Operations and advises that organization, its work and opinions do not necessarily reflect the position or views of the Argentine Navy.

CENTER FOR HEMISPHERIC STUDIES ALEXIS DE TOCQUEVILLE

The Center for Hemispheric Studies Alexis de Tocqueville is a private, nonaffiliated organization dedicated to the production of strategic analyses and action proposals with the intention of promoting better integration of the hemisphere. Headquartered in Buenos Aires, the Center's activities are concentrated on a mission to promote the generation of ideas that aim to create a set of strategic guidelines for countries of the region within an environment of deep political and philosophical consensus. This consensus must take into consideration key issues such as the consolidation of democracy, a common search for a hemispheric security framework, improvement in economic relationships, management and containment of social conflict, and the upholding of human rights.

The Center's programs are dedicated to exchanging and spreading ideas through the media, organization of open forums, and seminars in educational institutions, always promoting the involvement of students in research projects and conferences.

LATIN AMERICAN STUDIES GROUP OF THE U.S. NAVAL WAR COLLEGE

The Latin American Studies Group supports the Navy, the U.S. Southern Command, and other elements of the U.S. Government in the formulation and execution of programs and policy by providing strategic academic and research partnerships through the region. It joins those members of the teaching and research faculty and staff of the Naval War College, and interested students, who are engaged in scholarly topical work related to the Americas. Many of its members have lived, studied, or served in the region. Among the activities of the Latin American Studies Group are collaborative research on regional security issues, international war games, and an active program of lectures and seminars by Naval War College faculty in naval war colleges and other institutions in Latin America and the Caribbean.

Titles in the Series

"Are We Beasts?" Churchill and the Moral Question of World War II "Area Bombing," by Christopher C. Harmon (December 1991).

Toward a Pax Universalis: A Historical Critique of the National Military Strategy for the 1990s, by Lieutenant Colonel Gary W. Anderson, U.S. Marine Corps (April 1992).

The "New" Law of the Sea and the Law of Armed Conflict at Sea, by Horace B. Robertson, Jr. (October 1992).

Global War Game: The First Five Years, by Bud Hay and Bob Gile (June 1993).

Beyond Mahan: A Proposal for a U.S. Naval Strategy in the Twenty-First Century, by Colonel Gary W. Anderson, U.S. Marine Corps (August 1993).

The Burden of Trafalgar: Decisive Battle and Naval Strategic Expectations on the Eve of the First World War, by Jan S. Breemer (October 1993).

Mission in the East: The Building of an Army in a Democracy in the New German States, by Colonel Mark E. Victorson, U.S. Army (June 1994).

Physics and Metaphysics of Deterrence: The British Approach, by Myron A. Greenberg (December 1994).

A Doctrine Reader: The Navies of the United States, Great Britain, France, Italy, and Spain, by James J. Tritten and Vice Admiral Luigi Donolo, Italian Navy (Retired) (December 1995).

Chaos Theory: The Essentials for Military Applications, by Major Glenn E. James, U.S. Air Force (October 1996).

The International Legal Ramifications of United States Counter-Proliferation Strategy: Problems and Prospects, by Frank Gibson Goldman (April 1997).

What Color Helmet? Reforming Security Council Peacekeeping Mandates, by Myron H. Nordquist (August 1997).

Sailing New Seas, by Admiral J. Paul Reason, U.S. Navy, Commander-in-Chief, U.S. Atlantic Fleet, with David G. Freymann (March 1998).

Theater Ballistic Missile Defense from the Sea: Issues for the Maritime Component Commander, by Commander Charles C. Swicker, U.S. Navy (August 1998).

International Law and Naval War: The Effect of Marine Safety and Pollution Conventions during International Armed Conflict, by Dr. Sonja Ann Jozef Boelaert-Suominen (December 2000).

The Third Battle: Innovation in the U.S. Navy's Silent Cold War Struggle with Soviet Submarines, by Owen R. Cote, Jr. (2003).

The Limits of Transformation: Officer Attitudes toward the Revolution in Military Affairs, by Thomas G. Mahnken and James R. FitzSimonds (2003).

Military Transformation and the Defense Industry after Next: The Defense Industrial Implications of Network-Centric Warfare, by Peter J. Dombrowski, Eugene Gholz, and Andrew L. Ross (2003).

The Evolution of the U.S. Navy's Maritime Strategy, 1977–1986, by John B. Hattendorf (2004).

Global War Game: Second Series, 1984–1988, by Robert H. Gile (2004).